Cross Stitch
FAIRIES

Over 50 Enchanting Designs

D&C
David and Charles

A DAVID & CHARLES BOOK
Copyright © David & Charles Limited 2005, 2006

David & Charles is an F+W Publications Inc. company
4700 East Galbraith Road
Cincinnati, OH 45236

First published in the UK in 2005
First paperback edition 2006

Designs Copyright © Claire Crompton, Maria Diaz, Joan Elliott,
Lucie Heaton and Lesley Teare 2005, 2006
Text, photography and layout Copyright © David & Charles 2005. 2006

ISBN-13: 978-0-7153-1946-8 hardback
ISBN-10: 0-7153-1946-9 hardback

ISBN-13: 978-0-7153-2573-5 paperback
ISBN-10: 0-7153-2573-6 paperback

Executive editor   Cheryl Brown
Desk editor   Ame Verso
Art editor   Prudence Rogers
Project editor and chart preparation   Lin Clements
Photography   Kim Sayer and Karl Adamson

Printed in China by SNP Leefung
for David & Charles
Brunel House   Newton Abbot   Devon

Visit our website at www.davidandcharles.co.uk

David & Charles books are available from all good bookshops; alternatively
you can contact our Orderline on 0870 9908222 or write to us at FREEPOST
EX2 110, D&C Direct, Newton Abbot, TQ12 4ZZ (no stamp required UK only);
US customers call 800-289-0963 and Canadian customers call 800-840-5220.

Contents

Introduction

Fairies are magical, eternal, worldwide and a wonderful subject for cross stitch, as the designs in this new collection show. Fairy images are perfect for so many occasions: the fun of a birthday, the romance of a wedding, the joy of a new baby, the adventure of childhood – fairies bring magic to it all.

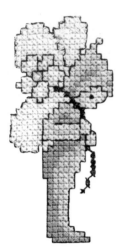

Fairy is an English word that originally meant 'to enchant', but over time has come to refer to a race of magical beings. Fairies as a general term often includes other mythical creatures like elves, fauns, brownies, dwarves, gnomes, goblins, leprechauns and pixies. The word too has many variations, including faery, fairye, fayerye and fayre. Ancient peoples believed that elemental spirits inhabited every hill, stream, tree

Ellefolk are Danish fairies living on moorland or in marshes, who tend beautiful gardens hidden in moss at forest edges.

and natural thing and this has given rise to beliefs in fairies as spirits of the earth, air, water and fire. Some folklorists think that the concept of fairies originated in ancient Greece and Italy, with the three Fates, goddesses who were thought to control the destinies of humankind and bestow gifts on the newborn – perhaps the origins of the fairy godmother? According to Greek myth, water nymphs inhabited all rivers, streams, lakes and pools. In the depths of the ocean dwelt sea fairies, as well as undines, mermaids and mermen, fey spirits who were believed to influence

Xindhi are Albanian elves, usually friendly towards humans but who are also capable of playing cruel tricks. A creaking door may announce their approach.

Yumboes are West African fairies that live under hills. They are served by attendants who are invisible except for their hands and feet.

the seas and weather. Dryads were land based, closely connected to trees, making their homes in them and living and dancing in woodland glades.

Fairy beliefs have been quite constant over many centuries. Fairies are recorded in Anglo-Saxon charms against elf arrows and are mentioned in some medieval manuscripts. Shakespeare of course used fairy tales and traditions frequently in his work, most famously in *A Midsummer-Night's Dream,* and many other poets and writers through the ages have drawn on fairy beliefs, including Homer, John Milton and William Blake.

Fairy tales have been hugely popular since Victorian times thanks to such writers as the Grimm

Menahune are Hawaiian fairies that emerge from the forest at night. They eat only raw vegetables and are excellent craftsmen.

brothers, Hans Christian Andersen, L. Frank Baum, Lewis Carroll and J. R. R. Tolkein. Indeed, some of our best-loved characters in literature, film and television have come from their imaginations – few of us have not heard of the naughty hobgoblin Puck, the brave bow-carrying elf Legolas or jealous little Tinkerbell.

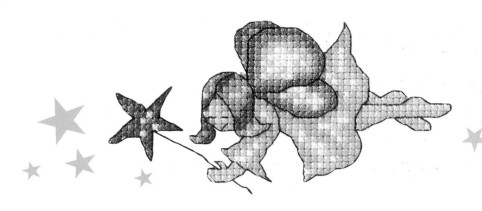

Feeorin are English fairies from Lancashire who love music and dancing and have been known to help humans. They usually have green skin and wear red caps.

The appearance of fairies varies greatly across the world and various cultures have described particular kinds of fairies in their folklore – pixies in England, elves in Germany, trolls in Scandinavia, jinni in the Middle East. Fairies in Western folklore, legend and fable were diminutive

Polevik are Russian cornfield fairies that grow with the grain. After harvest they shrink to hide among the last stalks of corn and claim any remaining grain.

supernatural beings with magical powers, mostly with a human shape and often with gauzy wings and this miniature nature spirit, popularized by Shakespeare and the Jacobean poets, has become a favourite Western image.

Fairies are thought to inhabit a realm that is rarely seen by humans although it co-exists with our world. In fairyland, fairies dance, feast and make merry, and humans who have found their way into this fantastical realm have found pleasure and excitement but also some danger, especially if they have eaten fairy food, which is said to enchant the unwary. Folk tales tell of people unable to leave fairyland or who pine away with a longing to return to it. Many artists have depicted scenes of the fairy realm, of fairy courts, dancing, revelry and romance,

particularly Victorian artists such as Richard Doyle, Henry Fuseli, John Simmons and Arthur Rackham.

The designers in this book have added to this wealth of imagery about fairies, producing distinctive, attractive and highly versatile designs you will find many uses for. Each chapter contains all you need to stitch the designs and make up the projects, with full step-by-step instructions and superb colour charts. At the end of the book is a short section on the equipment you will need and the basic techniques and stitches required. The designs are shown worked in DMC stranded cotton

Kelpie are Scottish water fairies who can appear as grey horses or as human men to seduce women. They can be detected by their hair, which looks like seaweed.

(floss) but for those of you who prefer Anchor threads there is a conversion table on page 102. There is also a good list of suppliers to help you find the exact materials and items used in the projects.

Fairyland is everywhere if we choose to look. This collection brings together many different fairy images – from the dreamily beautiful and delicate to the cute and cheeky. There is a fairy here to please everyone, so enter fairyland for a while and create a little magic of your own as you stitch these lovely designs.

Yakshas are nature fairies mostly found at wells and in the mountains in the magical kingdom of Alaka in the Himalayas. They guard treasure hidden under tree roots.

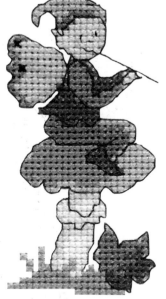

Designed by Joan Elliott

Garden Fairies

This wonderful hanging was inspired by the poem 'The Fairies' by Rose Fyleman that begins, 'There are fairies at the bottom of our garden.' These cute winged sprites embody many of our beliefs in fairies – their small size, their closeness with nature, their ability to remain hidden in plain sight. Folk tales say fairyland impinges on our world but is rarely seen, and entry to this magical place is only achieved under special circumstances or by the use of magical objects or herbs.

That fairies are close by in our gardens, sheltering under foxgloves and primroses and playing with butterflies is a fascinating idea and one that has been explored by many writers and artists, for example, Cicely Mary Barker's images of flower fairies.

Stitch this fabulous design and enter the fairy realm with these delightful little pixies peeping from colourful flowers and leaves.

6

Garden Fairies Wall Hanging

This delightful design uses whole and three-quarter cross stitch, backstitch and French knots, with a liberal sprinkling of beads and metallic threads for magical sparkle. It has been made up as a wall hanging but could be framed instead to make a wonderful picture.

Stitch count
225 x 168
Design size
40.8 x 30.5cm (16 x 12in)

Materials
14-count flax Aida (DMC code 738)
53 x 43cm (21 x 17in)

★

Tapestry needle size 24
and a beading needle

★

DMC stranded cotton (floss)
as listed in chart key

★

Kreinik Very Fine #4 Braid:
001HL silver; 5003 dragonfly
and 009 emerald (3 spools)

★

Kreinik Fine #8 Braid 022 brown

★

Kreinik Blending Filament
032 pearl (2 spools)

★

Mill Hill glass seed beads:
00374 rainbow; 02010 ice
and 02017 crystal aqua

★

Mill Hill antique glass beads
03047 blue iris

1 Prepare for work, referring to Techniques (page 99) if necessary. Find and mark the centre of the fabric and circle the centre of the chart with a pen. Use an embroidery frame if you wish.

2 Start stitching from the centre of the chart and fabric, using two strands of stranded cotton (floss) for full and three-quarter cross stitches. Use one strand for all Kreinik Very Fine #4 Braid cross stitches. Use one strand of Kreinik Fine #8 Braid 022 wrapped once around the needle for the French knots in the lettering. Use one strand of Kreinik Very Fine #4 braid wrapped once around the needle for 5003 and 002 French knots. Following the colour changes on the chart, use one strand of stranded cotton (floss) wrapped twice around the needle for all other French knots.

3 Work the backstitches in the colours indicated in the chart key. Backstitch the fairies wings using one strand of Kreinik Very Fine #4 Braid 001HL and one strand of DMC 938 together in the needle. Use one strand of stranded cotton (floss), Kreinik #4 or Kreinik #8 braids for all other backstitches.

4 The fairy wings have the addition of metallic blending filament. Working in one direction in half cross stitch, overstitch the completed DMC blanc, 677 and 3811 cross stitches in all the wings with one strand of Kreinik Blending Filament #032. Finally, attach the beads where indicated on the chart using a beading needle and matching thread (see Techniques page 100).

Making Up
Background fabric 0.5m (½yd)

★

Fusible fleece and fusible web
0.5m (½yd) each

★

Iron-on interfacing or thin wadding
(batting) 0.5m (½yd)

★

Decorative braid 2m (2yd)

★

Four decorative flowers or buttons

★

Permanent fabric glue

★

Wooden dowel 2.5cm (1in)
diameter x 47cm (18½in) long

★

Matching sewing thread

Inspiration

Stitch just a single pixie for a charming little card.

One fairy came in violet,
And one wore indigo;
In blue, green, yellow, orange, red,
They made a pretty row.

From 'The Rainbow Fairies' by Robert Graves (1895–1985)

Making Up as a Hanging

5 Once the stitching is complete, make up the wall hanging as follows: cut two 54.5 x 44.5cm (21½ x 17½in) pieces of background fabric plus three 15 x 10cm (6 x 4in) pieces for tabs.

6 Cut a 54.5 x 44.5cm (21½ x 17½in) piece of fusible fleece and fuse this to the wrong side of one of the fabric pieces, following the manufacturer's instructions. Position the embroidery on the right side of the fleece-lined fabric, sewing or fusing it on as follows:

Sewing the embroidery to fabric:
Use the fabric weave as a guide to trim to within twelve rows of the design. Fold the edges over by eight rows, leaving four showing. Press folds into place. To avoid the background fabric showing through the embroidery, cut wadding (batting) or felt the same size as the design and place behind the embroidery before stitching it down. Place the design and wadding on the fabric and machine or hand stitch it in place close to the edge, using the fabric weave as a guide.

Fusing the embroidery to fabric:
Trim and fold the finished embroidery as before. To avoid the background fabric showing through, cut a piece of medium-weight iron-on interfacing the same size as the design and insert it behind the embroidery. Use a press cloth to iron and fuse the pieces together from the wrong side, keeping the folded edges in place. Cut a piece of fusible web the same size as the prepared embroidery. Sandwich the web between the right side of the background fabric and the embroidery, making sure that no edges of fusible web are visible, trimming it if necessary. Pin or tack (baste) in place. Using a press cloth, fuse the layers according to the manufacturer's instructions.

7 Stitch or glue the length of decorative braid around the outer edge of the embroidery, starting and ending at the centre bottom, attaching one of the flowers or buttons where the ends meet.

8 To make the tabs, fold each piece of 15 x 10cm (6 x 4in) fabric in half lengthwise, right sides together. Sew a 1.25cm (½in) seam down the length and across one short end. Trim the seam, turn right side out and press. Now pin the tabs evenly across the top of the hanging with sewn ends pointing towards the centre and raw edges matching.

9 Place the second piece of background fabric on top, right side facing, and stitch a 1.25cm (½in) seam all around leaving a gap for turning. Turn right side out, press and slipstitch the gap. Bring the loose ends of the tabs to the front and sew a decorative flower or button on each end. Paint the dowel to complement the embroidery and when dry insert it through the tabs, ready for hanging.

Inspiration

Choose two smaller areas of the main design to create two delightful little framed pictures, ideal to adorn the nursery wall.

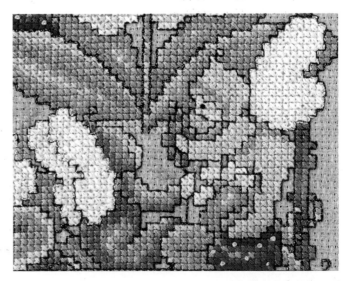

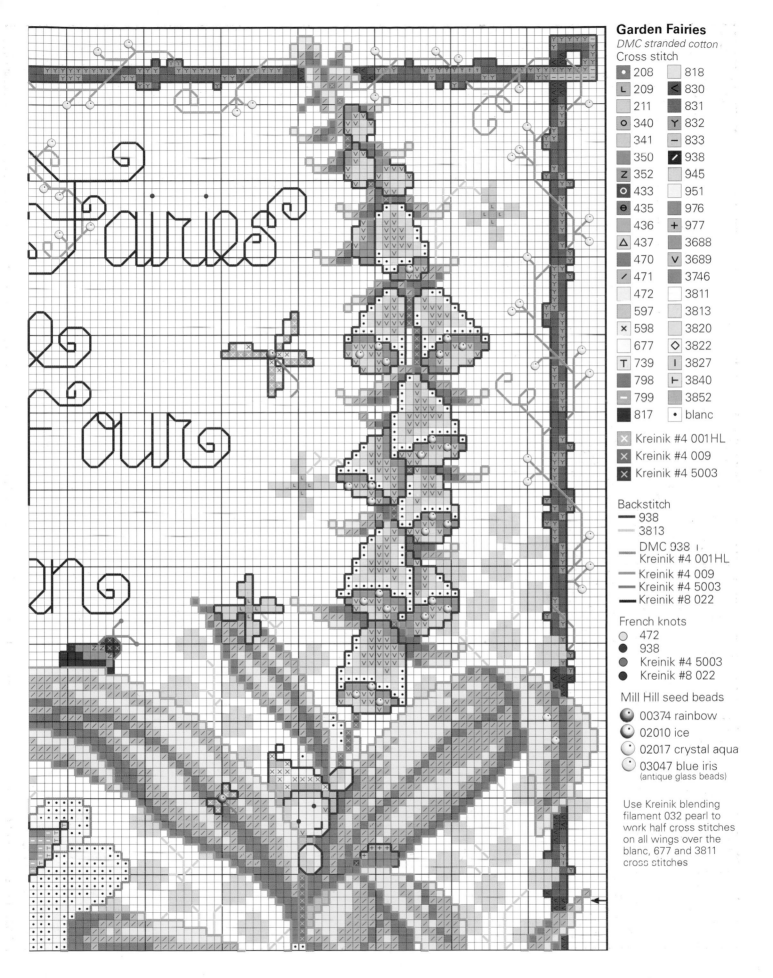

Garden Fairies

DMC stranded cotton

Cross stitch

⊙	208		818
L	209	<	830
	211		831
O	340	Y	832
	341	−	833
	350	⁄	938
Z	352		945
O	433		951
⊖	435		976
	436	+	977
△	437		3688
	470	V	3689
⁄	471		3746
	472		3811
	597		3813
×	598		3820
	677	◇	3822
T	739	I	3827
⊢	798	⊦	3840
−	799		3852
	817	•	blanc

⊠	Kreinik #4 001HL
⊠	Kreinik #4 009
⊠	Kreinik #4 5003

Backstitch

▬	938
▬	3813
▬	DMC 938 Kreinik #4 001HL
▬	Kreinik #4 009
▬	Kreinik #4 5003
▬	Kreinik #8 022

French knots

○	472
●	938
●	Kreinik #4 5003
●	Kreinik #8 022

Mill Hill seed beads

◐	00374 rainbow
○	02010 ice
○	02017 crystal aqua
⊙	03047 blue iris (antique glass beads)

Use Kreinik blending filament 032 pearl to work half cross stitches on all wings over the blanc, 677 and 3811 cross stitches

In emerald tufts, flowers purple, blue and white,
Like sapphire, pearl and rich embroidery,
Buckled below fair knighthood's bending knee.
Fairies use flowers for their charactery.

From *The Merry Wives of Windsor* by William Shakespeare (1564–1616)

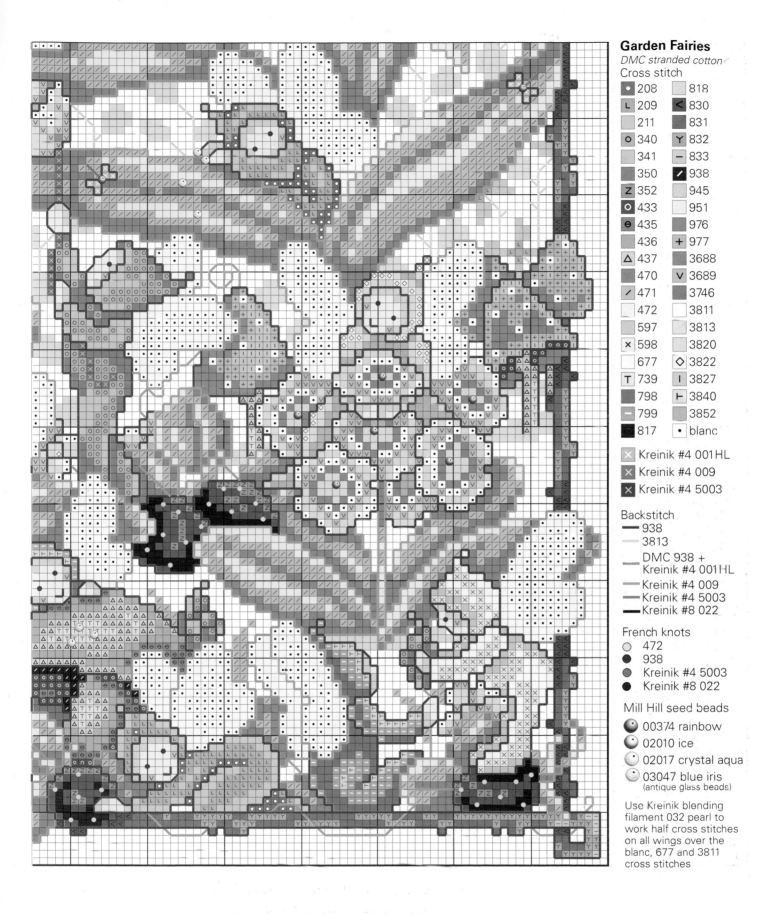

Garden Fairies
DMC stranded cotton
Cross stitch

◉	208		818
L	209	<	830
	211		831
O	340	Y	832
	341	–	833
	350	◢	938
Z	352		945
○	433		951
⊖	435		976
	436	+	977
△	437		3688
	470	V	3689
◢	471		3746
	472		3811
	597		3813
×	598		3820
	677	◇	3822
T	739	I	3827
	798	⊢	3840
–	799		3852
	817	•	blanc

⊠	Kreinik #4 001HL
⊠	Kreinik #4 009
⊠	Kreinik #4 5003

Backstitch
——	938
——	3813
----	DMC 938 + Kreinik #4 001HL
——	Kreinik #4 009
——	Kreinik #4 5003
——	Kreinik #8 022

French knots
○	472
●	938
⬤	Kreinik #4 5003
●	Kreinik #8 022

Mill Hill seed beads
◓	00374 rainbow
◔	02010 ice
◍	02017 crystal aqua
◑	03047 blue iris (antique glass beads)

Use Kreinik blending filament 032 pearl to work half cross stitches on all wings over the blanc, 677 and 3811 cross stitches

Designed by Maria Diaz

Birthday Fairies

Music and dancing are said to be favourite pastimes of fairies, and folk tales, literature and art are full of references to fairies dancing and playing instruments. Fairy rings – circles of mushrooms or bright green grass that appear on lawns and meadows – are said to reveal the places where fairies have spent the night dancing. Fairy music is unbearably sweet and compelling, able to draw humans into the magical ring and so into fairyland to dance all night – maybe never to return. The dancing fairy designs in this chapter are certainly very inviting. They have been designed as birthday cards to personify each month of the year, and are worked in stranded cotton (floss) with some metallic threads to create additional sparkle.

> **These lovely cards are perfect for birthdays and are versatile too – omit the month and insert a personal message instead for a really special card.**

14

Fairy Cards

These delightful fairies are simple to stitch using just full and three-quarter cross stitch, backstitch and some French knots. They have been stitched on 14-count Aida fabrics but you could use 28-count evenweaves instead if you prefer, stitching over two fabric threads instead of one block. The designs have been mounted into ready-

made cards (from Craft Creations, see Suppliers) but you could easily make you own cards – see page 30. Stitch the designs for birthdays or create a memorable keepsake by inserting a message of your own using an alphabet of your choice or the one on page 31. Alternatively, mount and frame the fairies as little pictures.

January

This elegant ballerina fairy of snowy white and icy mauve, stitched on navy Aida perfectly represents the cold first month of the year. The design would also make an attractive New Year card.

Stitch count
61 x 45

Design size
11 x 8cm (4⅜ x 3¼in)

Materials
14-count navy Aida
25 x 25cm (10 x 10in)

★

Tapestry needle size 24–26

★

DMC stranded cotton (floss)
as listed in chart key

★

Lilac double-fold card blank
with 12.2 x 9.6cm
(4¾ x 3¾in) oval aperture

★

Double-sided adhesive tape

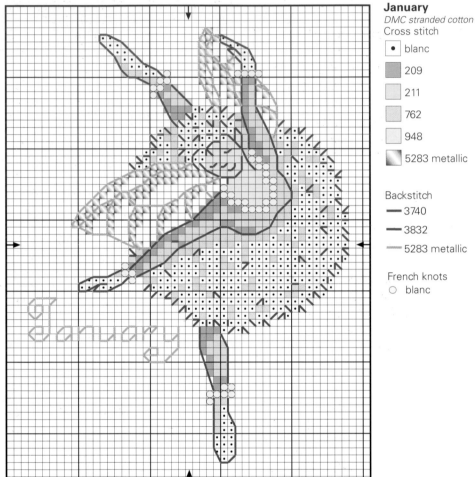

January
DMC stranded cotton
Cross stitch

•	blanc
▓	209
░	211
░	762
░	948
▨	5283 metallic

Backstitch
—— 3740
—— 3832
—— 5283 metallic

French knots
○ blanc

Prepare your fabric for work, mark the centre and begin stitching from the centre of the fabric and chart. Work over one block, using three strands of stranded cotton (floss) for cross stitch and French knots and one strand for backstitch. If you wish, you could personalize the design using the alphabet on page 31. Make a card (described on page 30) or buy a ready-made card and mount your embroidery in it (page 30).

February

This fairy is dressed in cool, frosty blues with an icicle skirt, colours that not only reflect this chilly month but also suit the watery star sign of Aquarius.

Stitch count
62 x 43

Design size
11.2 x 7.8cm (4½ x 3in)

Materials
14-count white Aida
25 x 25cm (10 x 10in)

★

Tapestry needle size 24–26

★

DMC stranded cotton (floss)
as listed in chart key

★

Silver double-fold card blank
with 12.2 x 9.6cm
(4¾ x 3¾in) aperture

★

Double-sided adhesive tape

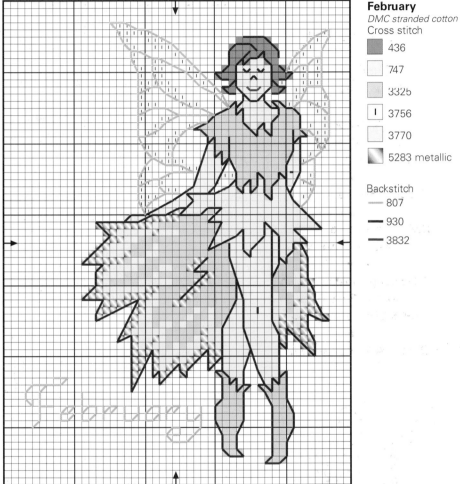

February
DMC stranded cotton
Cross stitch

▨	436
□	747
▨	3325
I	3756
□	3770
◩	5283 metallic

Backstitch

—	807
—	930
—	3832

Prepare your fabric for work, mark the centre and begin stitching from the centre of the fabric and chart. Work over one block, using two strands of stranded cotton (floss) for cross stitch and one strand for backstitch. If you wish, you could personalize the design using the alphabet on page 31. Make a card (described on page 30) or buy a ready-made card and mount your embroidery in it (page 30).

March

*This fairy is all in frothy spring greens, her skirts ruffled
up like a cancan dancer. The shamrock leaf is a reminder
that St Patrick's Day occurs in this month.*

Stitch count
58 x 44
Design size
10.5 x 8cm (4⅛ x 3⅛in)

Materials
14-count cream Aida
25 x 25cm (10 x 10in)
★
Tapestry needle size 24–26
★
DMC stranded cotton (floss)
as listed in chart key
★
Lime double-fold card blank
with 12.2 x 9.6cm
(4¾ x 3¾in) aperture
★
Double-sided adhesive tape

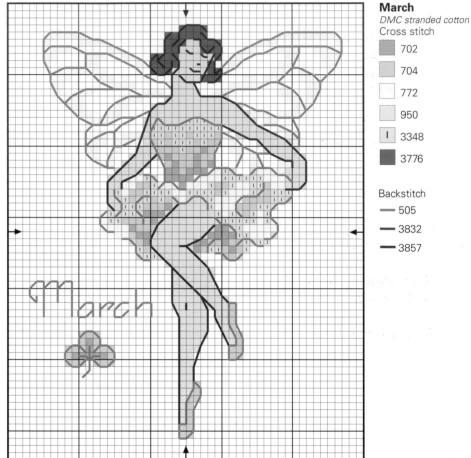

March
DMC stranded cotton
Cross stitch

	702
	704
	772
	950
I	3348
	3776

Backstitch
— 505
— 3832
— 3857

Prepare your fabric for work, mark the
centre and begin stitching from the
centre of the fabric and chart. Work
over one block, using two strands of
stranded cotton (floss) for cross stitch
and one strand for backstitch. If you wish,
you could personalize the design using
the alphabet on page 31. Make a card
(described on page 30) or buy a ready-
made card and mount your embroidery
in it (page 30).

April

An exuberant fairy in refreshing yellow dances through the spring showers of this month. This design would also be suitable for an Easter card, replacing the month with 'Happy Easter'.

Stitch count
52 x 54

Design size
9.4 x 9.8cm (3¾ x 3⅞in)

Materials
14-count ice blue Aida
25 x 25cm (10 x 10in)

★

Tapestry needle size 24–26

★

DMC stranded cotton (floss)
as listed in chart key

★

Gold single-fold card blank
14.5 x 19.8cm (5¾ x 7¾in)

★

Double-sided adhesive tape

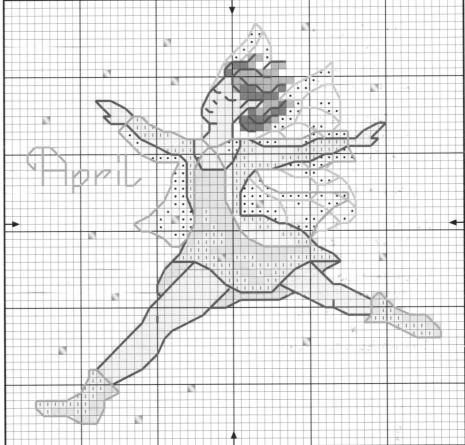

Prepare your fabric for work, mark the centre and begin stitching from the centre of the fabric and chart. Work over one block, using two strands of stranded cotton (floss) for cross stitch and one strand for backstitch. If you wish, you could personalize the design using the alphabet on page 31. Once the stitching is complete, fray the edges of the embroidery and stick it to the front of the card with double-sided adhesive tape (see page 31). Alternatively, make a double-fold card (described on page 30) and mount the design in it.

April
DMC stranded cotton

Cross stitch		Backstitch	
▓	435	——	741
▒	437	——	975
░	743	——	5284 metallic
I	744		
•	746		
	3078		
	3770		
▨	5284 metallic		

May

This fairy princess dances in the pretty lilacs and blues of late spring. The design would be perfect to congratulate a young girl on a task well done – simply replace the month with her name.

Stitch count
61 x 46
Design size
11 x 8.3cm (4⅜ x 3¼in)

Materials
14-count cream Aida
25 x 25cm (10 x 10in)
★
Tapestry needle size 24–26
★
DMC stranded cotton (floss)
as listed in chart key
★
Pale blue double-fold card blank
with 12.2 x 9.6cm
(4¾ x 3¾in) aperture
★
Double-sided adhesive tape

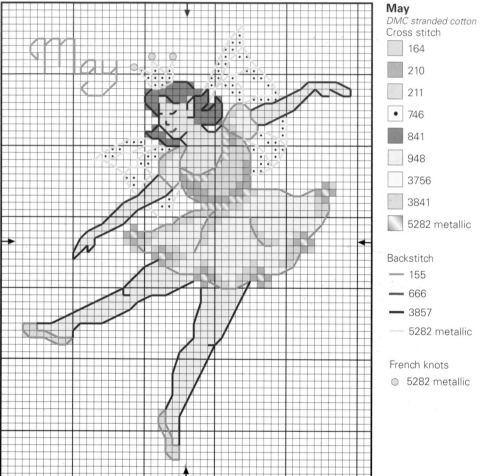

May
DMC stranded cotton
Cross stitch

	164
	210
	211
•	746
	841
	948
	3756
	3841
	5282 metallic

Backstitch

	155
	666
	3857
	5282 metallic

French knots

◯	5282 metallic

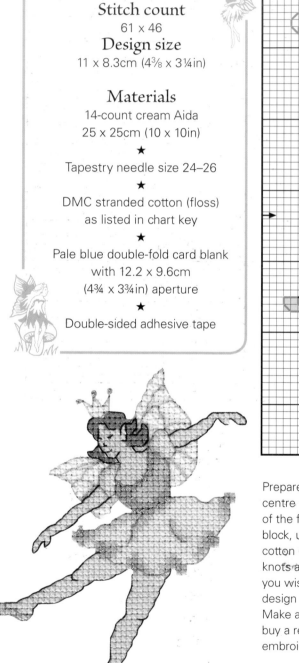

Prepare your fabric for work, mark the centre and begin stitching from the centre of the fabric and chart. Work over one block, using two strands of stranded cotton (floss) for cross stitch and French knots and one strand for backstitch. If you wish, you could personalize the design using the alphabet on page 31. Make a card (described on page 30) or buy a ready-made card and mount your embroidery in it (page 30).

June

*A demure little fairy in the floral pinks of early summer
makes a lovely June birthday card but could also be used
on a bridesmaid's gift such as a little keepsake bag.*

Stitch count
46 x 51

Design size
8.3 x 9.2cm (3¼ x 3⅝in)

Materials

14-count white Aida
25 x 25cm (10 x 10in)

★

Tapestry needle size 24–26

★

DMC stranded cotton (floss)
as listed in chart key

★

Lilac double-fold card blank
with 9.6 x 12.2cm
(3¾ x 4¾in) oval aperture

★

Double-sided adhesive tape

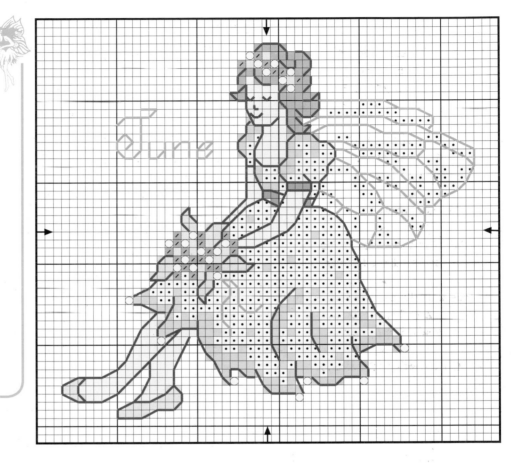

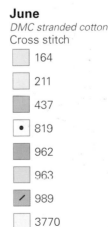

Prepare your fabric for work, mark
the centre and begin stitching
from the centre of the fabric
and chart. Work over one block,
using two strands of stranded
cotton (floss) for cross stitch
and French knots and one strand
for backstitch. If you wish, you could
personalize the design using the alphabet
on page 31. Make a card (described on
page 30) or buy a ready-made card and
mount your embroidery in it (page 30).

June
DMC stranded cotton

Cross stitch		Backstitch	
☐	164	—	962
☐	211	▬	3740
☐	437	▬	3832
•	819		
☐	962	French knots	
☐	963	○	3078
╱	989		
☐	3770		

July

In her red, white and blue costume, this fairy dancer celebrates American Independence Day on 4 July. This sunny month is represented by the yellow Aida and gold metallic thread.

Stitch count
61 x 44
Design size
11 x 8cm (4⅜ x 3⅛in)

Materials
14-count lemon Aida
25 x 25cm (10 x 10in)

★

Tapestry needle size 24–26

★

DMC stranded cotton (floss)
as listed in chart key

★

Dark blue double-fold card blank
with 12.2 x 9.6cm
(4¾ x 3¾in) aperture

★

Double-sided adhesive tape

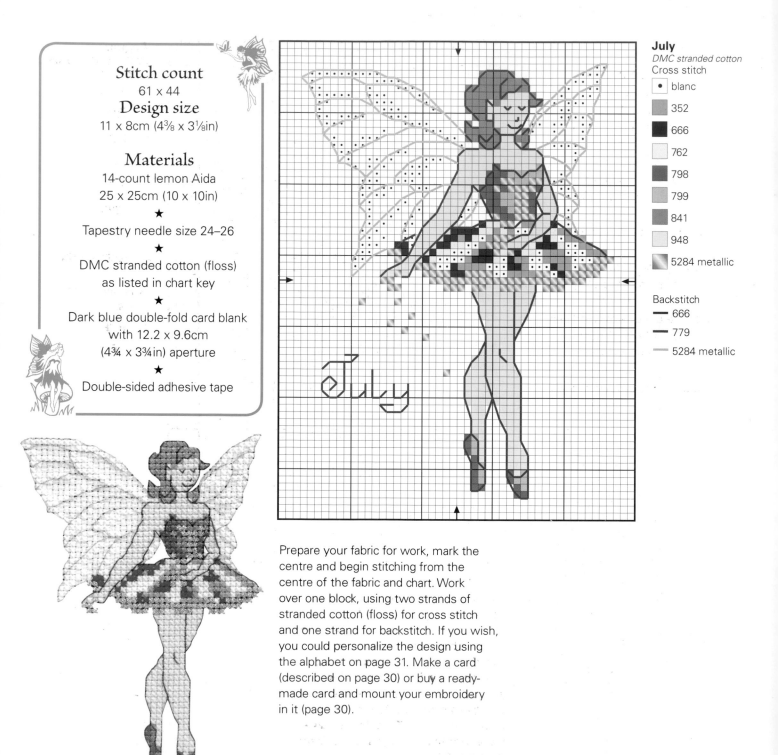

July
DMC stranded cotton
Cross stitch

- ● blanc
- 352
- 666
- 762
- 798
- 799
- 841
- 948
- 5284 metallic

Backstitch
— 666
— 779
— 5284 metallic

Prepare your fabric for work, mark the centre and begin stitching from the centre of the fabric and chart. Work over one block, using two strands of stranded cotton (floss) for cross stitch and one strand for backstitch. If you wish, you could personalize the design using the alphabet on page 31. Make a card (described on page 30) or buy a ready-made card and mount your embroidery in it (page 30).

August

This fairy is dressed ready for a day at the beach under the clear blue of a summer sky – perfect for a birthday in this cloudless month. The design would also make a great beach party invitation.

Stitch count
61 x 38

Design size
11 x 7cm (4⅜ x 2¾in)

Materials
14-count white Aida
25 x 25cm (10 x 10in)

★

Tapestry needle size 24–26

★

DMC stranded cotton (floss)
as listed in chart key

★

Pale blue double-fold card blank
with 12.2 x 9.6cm
(4¾ x 3¾in) oval aperture

★

Double-sided adhesive tape

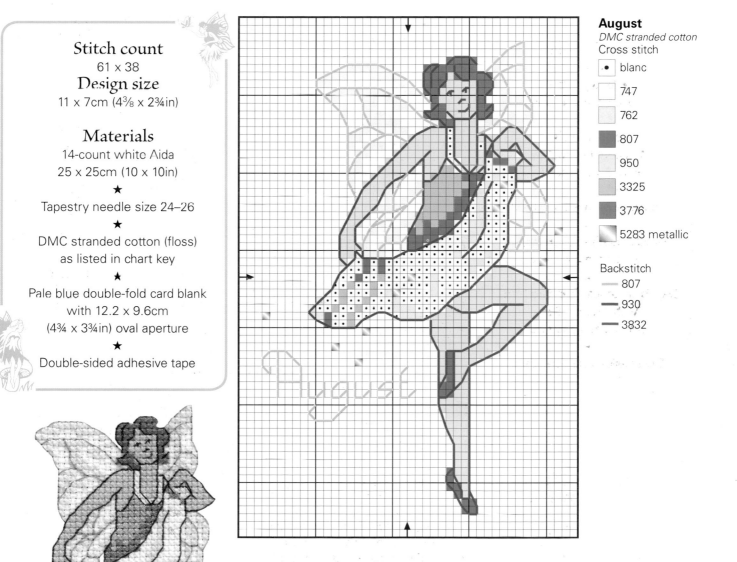

August
DMC stranded cotton
Cross stitch

·	blanc
	747
	762
	807
	950
	3325
	3776
	5283 metallic

Backstitch

—	807
—	930
—	3832

Prepare your fabric for work, mark the centre and begin stitching from the centre of the fabric and chart. Work over one block, using two strands of stranded cotton (floss) for cross stitch and one strand for backstitch. If you wish, you could personalize the design using the alphabet on page 31. Make a card (described on page 30) or buy a ready-made card and mount your embroidery in it (page 30).

September

This fairy's costume, with its cute sunflower-petal skirt, perfectly captures early autumn with all of its warm gold, orange and russet colours.

Stitch count
62 x 50
Design size
11.2 x 9cm (4½ x 3½in)

Materials
14-count ecru Aida
25 x 25cm (10 x 10in)
★
Tapestry needle size 24–26
★
DMC stranded cotton (floss)
as listed in chart key
★
Gold double-fold card blank
with 12.2 x 9.6cm
(4¾ x 3¾in) aperture
★
Double-sided adhesive tape

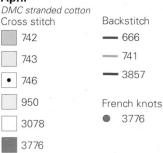

Prepare your fabric for work, mark the centre and begin stitching from the centre of the fabric and chart. Work over one block, using two strands of stranded cotton (floss) for cross stitch and French knots and one strand for backstitch. If you wish, you could personalize the design using the alphabet on page 31. Make a card (described on page 30) or buy a ready-made card and mount your embroidery in it (page 30).

April
DMC stranded cotton

Cross stitch		Backstitch	
▨	742	—	666
▨	743	—	741
•	746	—	3857
▨	950		
☐	3078	**French knots**	
▨	3776	●	3776

October

*With her costume of autumn foliage, this fairy celebrates an
October birthday with exuberance, scattering leaves as she dances.
Work the design on black Aida for a dramatic Hallowe'en card.*

Stitch count
45 x 61
Design size
8 x 11cm (3¼ x 4⅜in)

Materials
14-count antique Aida
25 x 25cm (10 x 10in)
★
Tapestry needle size 24–26
★
DMC stranded cotton (floss)
as listed in chart key
★
Gold double-fold card blank
with 9.6 x 12.2cm
(3¾ x 4¾in) aperture
★
Double-sided adhesive tape

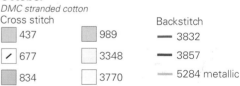

October
DMC stranded cotton
Cross stitch

Cross stitch		Backstitch	
▦ 437	▨ 989	— 3832	
╱ 677	▢ 3348	— 3857	
▨ 834	▢ 3770	— 5284 metallic	

Prepare your fabric for work, mark the
centre and begin stitching from the centre
of the fabric and chart. Work over one
block, using three strands of stranded
cotton (floss) for cross stitch and one
strand for backstitch. If you wish, you could
personalize the design using the alphabet
on page 31. Make a card (described on
page 30) or buy a ready-made card and
mount your embroidery in it (page 30).

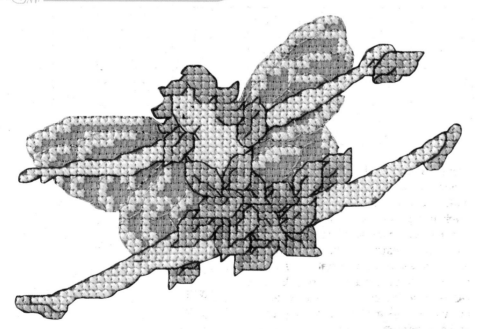

November

This fairy dancer in orange, red and black is as
exciting as a bonfire. The design would also make
a very atmospheric fireworks party invitation.

Stitch count
61 x 50
Design size
11 x 9cm (4⅜ x 3½in)

Materials
14-count antique green Aida
25 x 25cm (10 x 10in)

★

Tapestry needle size 24–26

★

DMC stranded cotton (floss)
as listed in chart key

★

Orange double-fold card blank
with 12.2 x 9.6cm
(4¾ x 3¾in) aperture

★

Double-sided adhesive tape

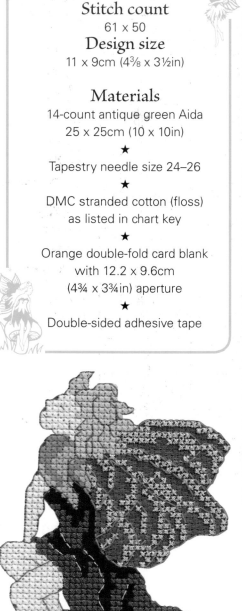

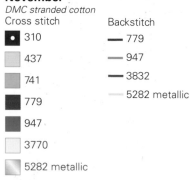

Prepare your fabric for work, mark the
centre and begin stitching from the
centre of the fabric and chart. Work
over one block, using three strands of
stranded cotton (floss) for cross stitch
and one strand for backstitch. If you wish,
you could personalize the design using
the alphabet on page 31. Make a card
(described on page 30) or buy a ready-
made card and mount your embroidery
in it (page 30).

November
DMC stranded cotton
Cross stitch

- ⬛• 310
- ⬜ 437
- ▦ 741
- ⬛ 779
- ▦ 947
- ⬜ 3770
- ▨ 5282 metallic

Backstitch
- — 779
- — 947
- — 3832
- — 5282 metallic

December

*This lovely fairy in Christmas red and sprigs of festive holly
is stitched on a very dark green Aida and would be perfect
for a December birthday or a pretty Christmas card.*

Stitch count
63 x 47
Design size
11.5 x 8.5cm (4½ x 3⅜in)

Materials
14-count moss green Aida
25 x 25cm (10 x 10in)

★

Tapestry needle size 24–26

★

DMC stranded cotton (floss)
as listed in chart key

★

Red double-fold card blank
with 12.2 x 9.6cm
(4¾ x 3¾in) aperture

★

Double-sided adhesive tape

December
DMC stranded cotton
Cross stitch
- ● blanc
- 164
- 437
- 498
- 666
- 948
- 989
- 5283 metallic

Backstitch
— 3857
— 666
— 5283 metallic

French knots
- ● 666

Prepare your fabric for work, mark the
centre and begin stitching from the centre
of the fabric and chart. Work over one
block, using three strands of stranded
cotton (floss) for cross stitch and French
knots and one strand for backstitch. If
you wish, you could personalize the
design using the alphabet on page 31.
Make a card (described on page 30) or
buy a ready-made card and mount your
embroidery in it (page 30).

Making an Aperture Card

1 Choose a card colour to complement your embroidery and cut a rectangle 15.9 x 43.3cm (6¼ x 18¾in), as shown in the diagram on page 31. On the wrong side of the card, draw two lines dividing it into three sections of 15.9cm (6¼in). Score gently along each line with the back of a craft knife to make folding easier.

2 In the centre section, mark an aperture slightly smaller than your embroidery, leaving a border of 2.2cm (⅞in) on all sides. Cut out the aperture with a sharp craft knife, carefully cutting into the corners neatly. (You could use a decorative cutter if you wish.) Trim the left edge of the first section by 2mm (⅛in) so that it lies flat when folded over to the inside of the card. This will cover the back of the stitching. Fold the left and then the right section on the scored lines.

Mounting an Embroidery into a Double-Fold Card

1 Lay the card right side up on top of the embroidered design so the stitching is in the middle of the aperture. Place a pin in each corner and remove the card. Trim the fabric to within about 1.5cm (⅝in) so it fits into the card.

2 On the wrong side of the card, stick double-sided tape around the aperture and peel off the backing tape. Place the card over the design, using the pins as a guide to position. Press down firmly so the fabric is stuck securely to the card.

3 On the wrong side of the card, stick more double-sided tape around the edge of the middle section. Peel off the backing tape, fold the left section in to cover the back of the stitching and press down firmly.

If you wish to add wadding (batting) to give a padded look to your embroidery, stick a piece into position, on the back of the embroidery, before pressing the middle card section into place.

If you see a faery ring
In a field of grass,
Very lightly step around,
Tip-toe as you pass,
Last night faeries frolicked there
And they're sleeping somewhere near.

'If You See a Fairy Ring' by William Shakespeare (1564–1616)

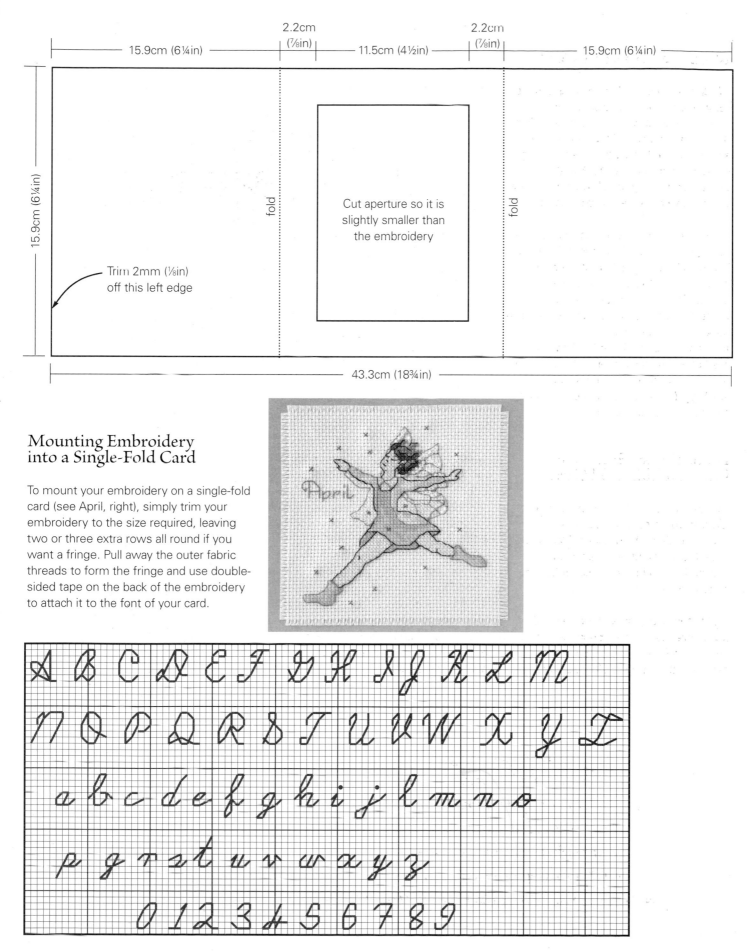

2.2cm (⅞in) 2.2cm (⅞in)

15.9cm (6¼in)   11.5cm (4½in)   15.9cm (6¼in)

15.9cm (6¼in)

fold

fold

Cut aperture so it is slightly smaller than the embroidery

Trim 2mm (⅛in) off this left edge

43.3cm (18¾in)

Mounting Embroidery into a Single-Fold Card

To mount your embroidery on a single-fold card (see April, right), simply trim your embroidery to the size required, leaving two or three extra rows all round if you want a fringe. Pull away the outer fabric threads to form the fringe and use double-sided tape on the back of the embroidery to attach it to the font of your card.

Personalize your cards with this alphabet or another of your choice – see page 63 for advice

Designed by Lesley Teare

Fairy Princess

In Western children's stories, fairies are often portrayed as tiny, winged creatures, such as Tinkerbell in *Peter Pan*, and Thumbelina in the Hans Christian Andersen story. However, across cultures their appearance varies widely. Fairies are described as having many diverse shapes and sizes: some are as tiny as insects, others as large as giants; some are invisible while others can change shape or disguise themselves.

This lovely fairy princess gleaming with shiny metallic threads and glass beads is sure to bring a romantic touch to any room.

This fairy is the epitome of sweet delicacy and beauty, with a touch of royalty about her. The concept of an alluring fairy queen, such as Shakespeare's Titania, has persisted for centuries in the popular imagination and this fairy design echoes that idea beautifully.

Fairy Princess Picture

This beautiful and romantic design of a fairy princess is sure to give much pleasure as you stitch it. It uses whole and three-quarter cross stitch, backstitch and long stitch with the addition of glittering metallic blending filaments and glass beads. The design could also be worked on a 14-count Aida fabric.

Stitch count
178 x 160

Design size
32 x 29cm (12¾ x 11½in)

Materials
28-count Quaker evenweave linen in Colonial blue, 46 x 41cm (18 x 16in)

★

Tapestry needle size 24–26

★

DMC stranded cotton (floss) as listed in chart key

★

Kreinik Blending Filament (BF), sky blue 014

★

Kreinik Very Fine (#4) Braid: white 100; gold dust 210; gold 002 and gold 002HL

★

Mill Hill glass seed beads, 00557 gold

★

Mount board, approx 46 x 41cm (18 x 16in)

★

Wadding (batting), approx 46 x 41cm (18 x 16in)

★

Double-sided adhesive tape

★

Pins

★

Crochet cotton or strong thread

★

Suitable picture frame

1 Prepare the fabric for work, finding and marking the centre (see page 99). Mount the fabric in an embroidery frame if you wish. Begin stitching from the centre of the fabric and the centre of the chart.

2 Work over two linen threads (or one block of Aida) using two strands of stranded cotton (floss) for full and three-quarter cross stitches and one strand for backstitches. Where the chart requires blending filament, use one strand of cotton and one strand of blending filament together in the needle. Use one strand of Very Fine (#4) Braid for the whole cross stitches and backstitches on the wings. Complete all cross stitches before working backstitches, long stitches and beading. Because of the number of colour changes it is a good idea to keep several needles threaded with different colours.

3 Work long stitches for the stars in one strand of Very Fine (#4) Braid gold 002HL. Use the same thread to attach beads with half cross stitches (page 100).

4 When all the stitching is complete, remove from the embroidery frame. Press the work wrong side down on thick towels with a cool iron, taking extra care with the metallic threads and beads.

Framing the Picture

5 Cut your mount board to the size of the picture frame aperture. Cut a piece of wadding (batting) the same size and secure it to the mount board with strips of double-sided adhesive tape.

6 Lay your embroidery face up on the wadding (batting) and when you are happy with the position, push a line of pins down each side into the board. Check the stitching is straight then trim the fabric to leave 5cm (2in) all round.

7 Fold the excess fabric to the back. Thread a needle with a long length of crochet cotton or strong thread, knot the end and lace the two opposite sides together on the back, starting at one end and working in an under-and-over motion, pulling the lacing tight. When you reach the other end, adjust the laced threads one by one before finishing off. Repeat this process on the two remaining edges.

8 Fold down the corners at the back and stitch neatly in place. Remove the pins and assemble your work in its frame.

Inspiration
The fairy princess would make a lovely nightdress case. You could either attach it as a patch to a plain case or stitch the design on the top third of a piece of Aida or linen, which can then be made up as a simple flap bag.

I met a lady in the meads
Full beautiful, a fairy's child
Her hair was long
Her foot was light
And her eyes were wild.

From 'La Belle Dame Sans Morci' by John Keats (1795–1821)

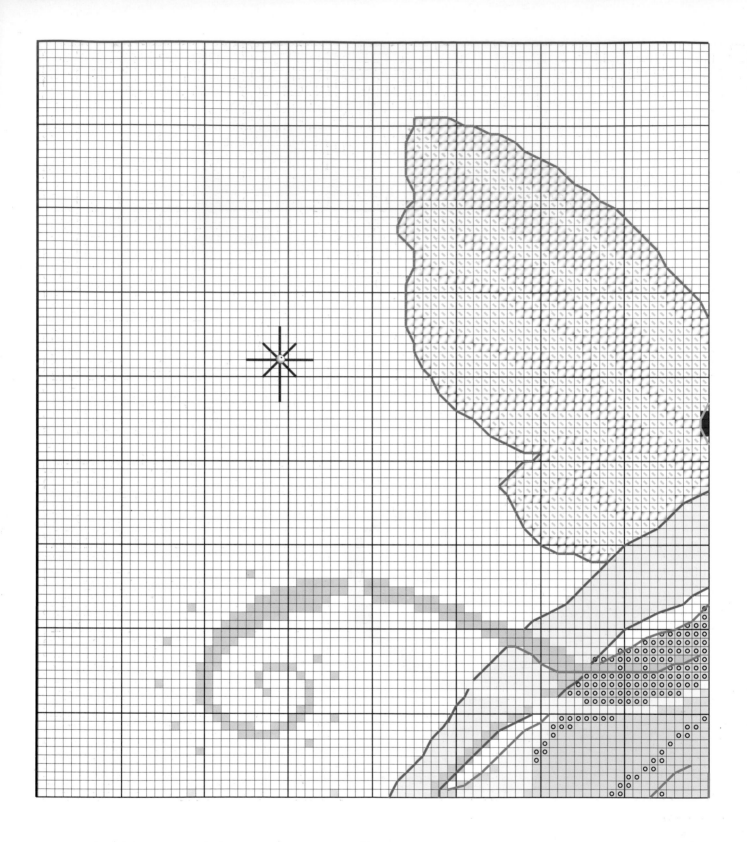

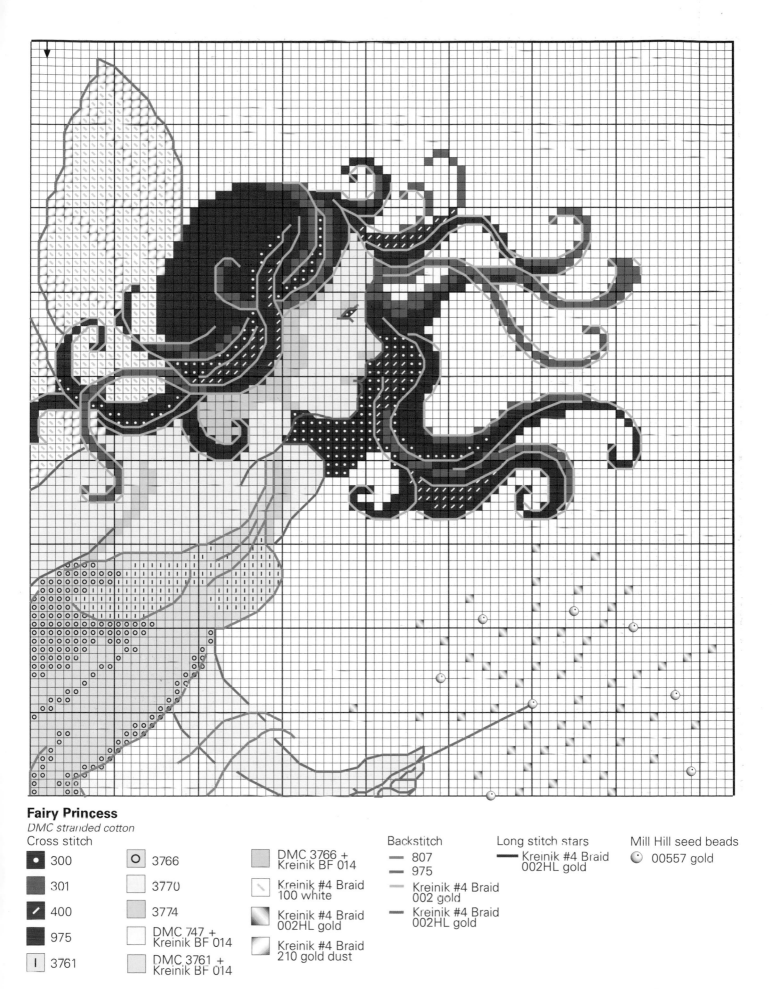

Fairy Princess

DMC stranded cotton

Cross stitch

300	3766	DMC 3766 + Kreinik BF 014	
301	3770	Kreinik #4 Braid 100 white	
400	3774	DMC 747 + Kreinik BF 014	
975		Kreinik #4 Braid 002HL gold	
3761	DMC 3761 + Kreinik BF 014	Kreinik #4 Braid 210 gold dust	

Backstitch
— 807
— 975
— Kreinik #4 Braid 002 gold
— Kreinik #4 Braid 002HL gold

Long stitch stars
— Kreinik #4 Braid 002HL gold

Mill Hill seed beads
◉ 00557 gold

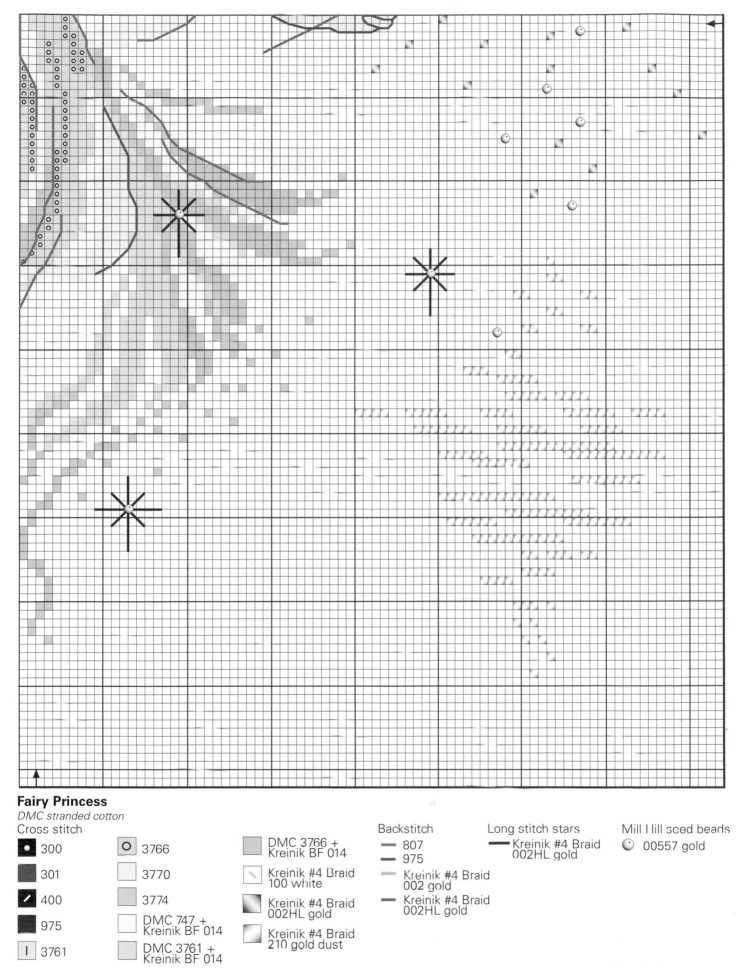

Fairy Princess

DMC stranded cotton

Cross stitch

● 300	○ 3766	▨ DMC 3766 + Kreinik BF 014
▨ 301	□ 3770	◥ Kreinik #4 Braid 100 white
◿ 400	▨ 3774	◼ Kreinik #4 Braid 002HL gold
▨ 975	□ DMC 747 + Kreinik BF 014	◥ Kreinik #4 Braid 210 gold dust
I 3761	□ DMC 3761 + Kreinik BF 014	

Backstitch
— 807
— 975
— Kreinik #4 Braid 002 gold
— Kreinik #4 Braid 002HL gold

Long stitch stars
— Kreinik #4 Braid 002HL gold

Mill Hill seed beads
☺ 00557 gold

Fairy Princess **39**

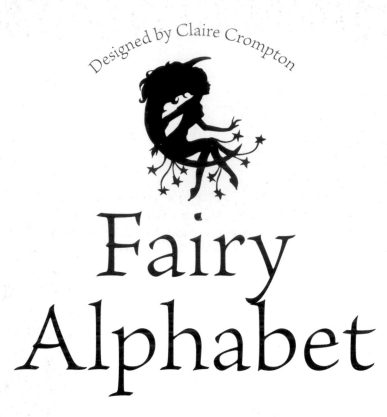

Designed by Claire Crompton

Fairy Alphabet

In the past it was considered unlucky to use a fairy's name because this could be considered a summons or even a challenge, and although in folklore many fairies were helpful to humans, often bringing gifts or doing housework, they were also easily offended.

Brownies – solitary fairies who attached themselves to a family and worked around the house – often went off in a huff if offered any reward. Accordingly, fairies were referred to by respectful names such as the good people, the wee folk, the hidden people, the hill folk or even just 'them' or 'themselves'. These little fairies are so sweet however, we're sure they won't mind at all if you use their delightful designs to create your own names and messages.

What better way to make a feature of a loved one's name or initial than with this charming fairy alphabet? Some of the letters are made up here as a card, picture and pot.

Fairies A to Z

This adorable fairy alphabet is simple to stitch using whole cross stitches, backstitches and French knots, yet creates such a pretty effect, as shown by this picture, card and trinket pot (overleaf). See how many more items and gifts you can grace with these delightful little fairies.

Stitch count
Each letter 53 x 49 max
Design size
Each letter 9.6 x 8.4cm
(3¾ x 3½in) max

Materials for each letter
14-count Aida or 28-count linen
in antique white, at least
20 x 18cm (8 x 7in)

★

Tapestry needle size 26

★

DMC stranded cotton (floss)
as listed in chart key

1 Prepare the fabric for work and mark the centre (see page 99). Mount the fabric in an embroidery hoop or frame if you wish and start stitching from the centre of the fabric and the centre of the chart (pages 45–51). Please note: a single key has been used for the whole alphabet but you will not need all the colours for every letter – check before you start.

2 Work over one block of Aida or over two linen threads, using two strands of stranded cotton (floss) for cross stitches and one for backstitches. Work the French knots with two strands wound twice around the needle. If stitching several fairies to create a name, it is best to plan the complete design on graph paper first so you can decide exactly where to place each letter, making sure the bottoms of the letters are level.

3 Once all the stitching is complete, take it out of the hoop if you have used one and press gently on the wrong side on a thick towel. The embroidery is now ready to be framed (see page 34), made up into a card (page 30) or mounted into a trinket pot lid (page 44).

Inspiration
Use the fairy alphabet to create a pretty gift bag. Stitch an initial on evenweave fabric, hem the edges and sew on to a ready-made bag, perhaps adding braid or twisted cord around the edges of the embroidery.

Some to the sun, their insect-wings unfold,
Waft on the breeze, or sink in clouds of gold,
Transparent forms, too fine for mortal sight,
Their fluid bodies half dissolved in light.

From 'The Rape of the Lock'
by Alexander Pope (1688–1744)

Making Up as a Picture

There is a wide variety of interesting and attractive ready-made frames and mounts available today, from all sorts of retail outlets. Detailed instructions for mounting embroidery into a picture frame can be found on page 34. For a totally individual look, you could customize your frame to suit your fairy picture: there are now paints with pearlescent, metallic or textured finishes and others that contain glitter.

Making Up into a Card

Ready-made cards are widely available from needlecraft shops and mail-order companies so it should be easy to choose one that complements your fairy design. If you are using a dark card colour and a light fabric, stick a piece of white paper to the left-hand flap of the card to stop the dark card showing through the embroidery.

To mount the embroidery into a card, first trim the embroidery so it is slightly larger than the card aperture and then use strips of double-sided adhesive tape to secure the fabric on to the card (see page 30 for more detailed instructions). For an extra special look you could decorate your card with ribbon, braid or paint effects.

A little fairy comes at night,
Her eyes are blue, her hair is brown,
With silver spots upon her wings,
And from the moon she flutters down.

'Dream Fairy' by Thomas Hood (1799–1845)

Mounting in a Trinket Pot

Trinket pots or boxes are perfect for displaying small embroideries like these and make lovely gifts (see Suppliers on page 103 for some addresses). Cut the embroidery to fit the trinket pot lid and assemble following the manufacturer's instructions, adding a piece of wadding (batting) under the embroidery to create a nice padded effect.

Inspiration

Use the fairy alphabet to create a lovely pillow for a girl's bedroom, stitching her name on either 14-count Aida or 28-count linen. Add a pretty fabric border around the embroidery and frothy, gathered lace around the edges when making up the pillow.

Inspiration

Stitch a fairy initial using gleaming metallic blending filaments combined with stranded cotton (floss) for an extra special sparkle, and then make up into a heart-shaped sachet filled with sweet-smelling pot-pourri.

Do you believe in fairies? Say quick that you believe!
If you believe, clap your hands.

From *Peter Pan* by Sir James M. Barrie (1860–1937)

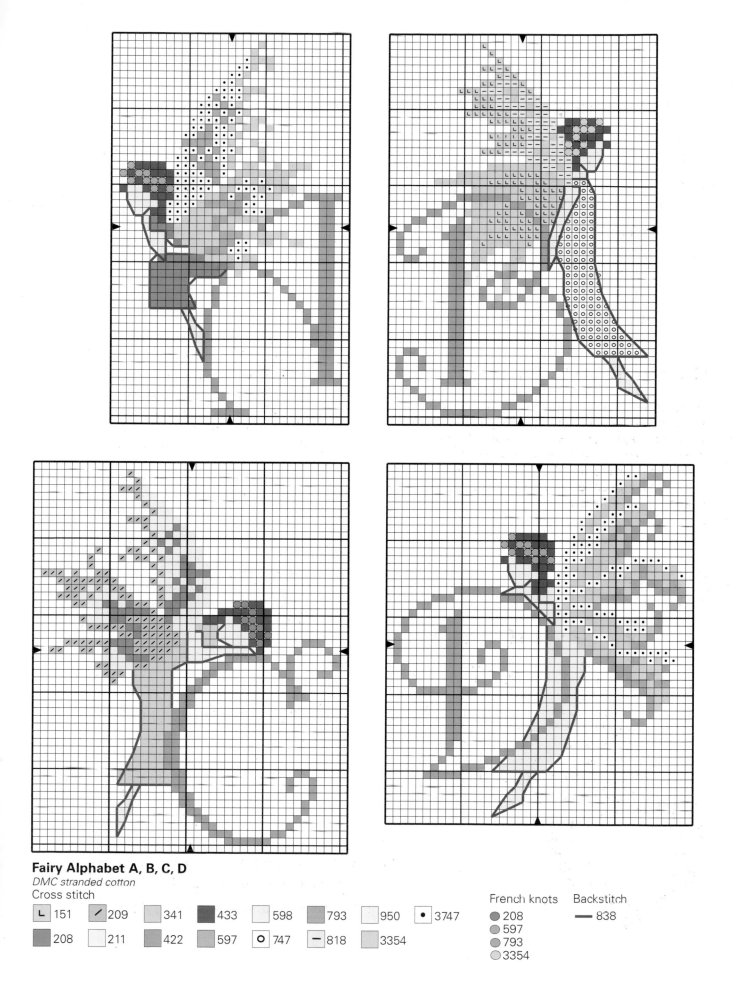

Fairy Alphabet A, B, C, D
DMC stranded cotton
Cross stitch

L 151	/ 209	341	433	598	793	950	• 3747
208	211	422	597	O 747	— 818	3354	

French knots
- 208
- 597
- 793
- 3354

Backstitch
— 838

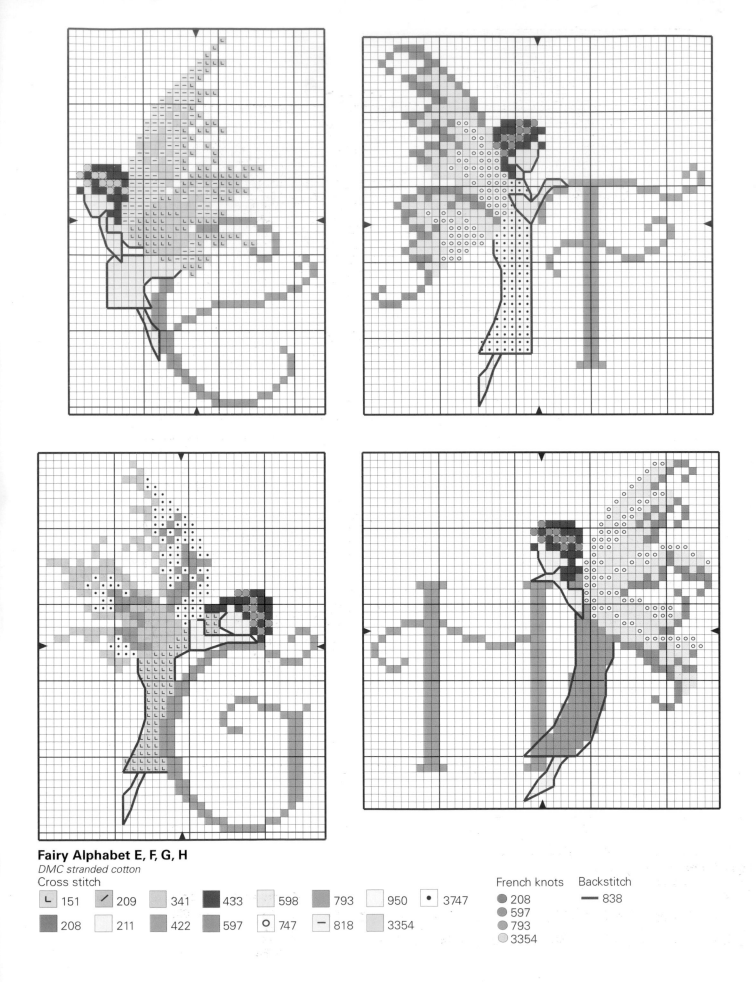

Fairy Alphabet E, F, G, H
DMC stranded cotton
Cross stitch

L 151	╱ 209	341	433	598	793	950	• 3747
208	211	422	597	O 747	— 818	3354	

French knots
- 208
- 597
- 793
- 3354

Backstitch
— 838

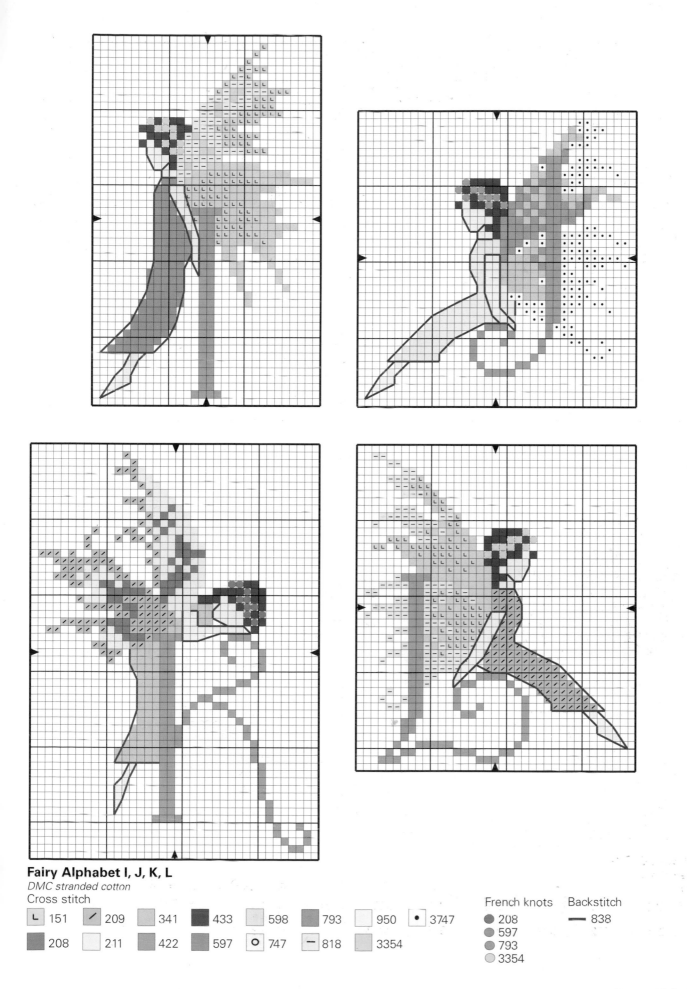

Fairy Alphabet I, J, K, L
DMC stranded cotton
Cross stitch

L 151	/ 209	341	433	598	793	950	• 3747
208	211	422	597	O 747	– 818	3354	

French knots
● 208
● 597
● 793
● 3354

Backstitch
— 838

Fairy Alphabet M, N, O, P
DMC stranded cotton
Cross stitch

L 151	⁄ 209	341	433	598	793	950	• 3747		
208	211	422	597	O 747	— 818	3354			

French knots
● 208
● 597
● 793
● 3354

Backstitch
— 838

Fairy Alphabet Q, R, S, T

DMC stranded cotton

Cross stitch

L 151	/ 209	341	433	598	793	950	• 3747
208	211	422	597	O 747	− 818	3354

French knots
- 208
- 597
- 793
- 3354

Backstitch
— 838

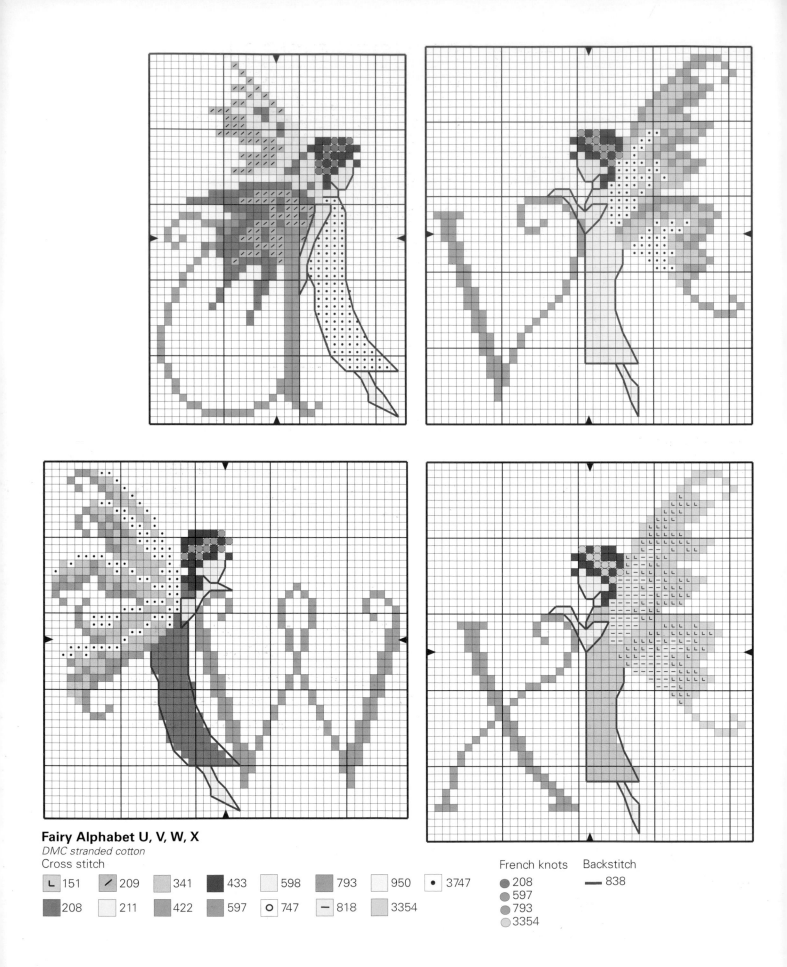

Fairy Alphabet U, V, W, X
DMC stranded cotton
Cross stitch

∟ 151	╱ 209	341	433	598	793	950	• 3747	
208	211	422	597	○ 747	— 818	3354		

French knots
● 208
● 597
● 793
● 3354

Backstitch
— 838

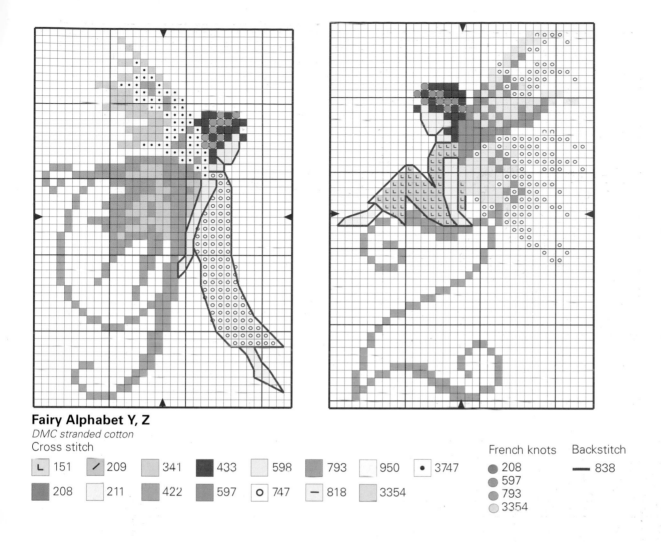

Fairy Alphabet Y, Z
DMC stranded cotton
Cross stitch

L	151	✓ 209	341	433	598	793	950	• 3747		
	208	211	422	597	O 747	— 818	3354			

French knots
● 208
● 597
● 793
○ 3354

Backstitch
— 838

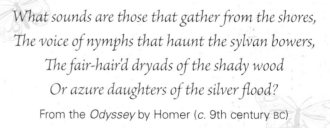

What sounds are those that gather from the shores,
The voice of nymphs that haunt the sylvan bowers,
The fair-hair'd dryads of the shady wood
Or azure daughters of the silver flood?

From the *Odyssey* by Homer (*c.* 9th century BC)

Designed by Lucie Heaton

Nursery Fairies

It's hard to imagine a nursery or child's room today that doesn't feature characters from fairy tales and nursery rhymes. Tales of magic and enchantment became immensely popular during the Victorian era as an educational tool, particularly Aesop's fables and the stories of Hans Christian Andersen and the Grimm brothers, ensuring that generations of children came to know and love the little mermaid, Rapunzel, Tom Thumb, Hansel and Gretel and many more. For more than 80 years film studios have brought other stories to magical life, such as *Snow White and the Seven Dwarfs*, *The Wizard of Oz*, *Peter Pan* and *The Lord of the Rings*. The designs in this chapter feature toy-like fairies reminiscent of those old stories but with a modern twist.

Bring fairy tale magic into the nursery with four delightful designs – a birth sampler, album, card and a pillow that is sure to invite the mysterious tooth fairy to visit.

52

When the first baby laughed

for the

first time....

Emma Jane
6th April
2004

that was

the beginning

of fairies.....

Fairy Birth Sampler

This delightful sampler with its cheeky fairies and elves would make a wonderful memento of the birth of a baby. The lovely quotation is from that eternal favourite Peter Pan. The sampler is simplicity itself to stitch, using cross stitch, backstitch and French knots. It could also be worked over two threads of a 28-count evenweave.

Stitch count
140 x 98
Finished size
25.5 x 18cm (10 x 7in)

Materials
14-count white Aida
40 x 33cm (16 x 13in)

★

Tapestry needle size 24-26

★

DMC stranded cotton (floss)
as listed in chart key

★

Lightweight iron-on interfacing,
approx 40 x 33cm (16 x 13in)

★

Double-sided adhesive tape

★

Self-adhesive mount board,
approx 29 x 21.5cm
(11½ x 8½in)

1 Prepare the fabric for work, finding and marking the centre (see page 99). Mount the fabric in an embroidery frame if you wish. Begin stitching from the centre of the fabric and chart on pages 58–59.

2 Work over one block of Aida, using two strands of stranded cotton (floss) for cross stitch and French knots and one strand for backstitch.

3 To personalize the design, follow the instructions on page 63.

4 When all the stitching is complete, apply lightweight iron-on interfacing to the back of the embroidery, fusing in place with a medium iron. Remove the backing from the adhesive mount board, carefully centre the sampler on the board and press down firmly. Fold over the excess fabric and secure to the back of the board using double-sided tape or masking tape.

5 Your birth sampler is now ready for mounting and framing (see the instructions on page 34).

When the first baby laughed for the first time, the laugh broke into a thousand pieces and they all went skipping about, and that was the beginning of fairies.

From *Peter Pan* by Sir James M. Barrie
(1860–1937)

New Baby Card

This adorable little fairy, with her magic wand bringing good
fortune and precious gifts, is perfect for a card to welcome a new baby.
The design would also make a lovely door hanger for the nursery –
simply replace the words with the baby's name.

Stitch count
37 x 56
Finished size
6.7 x 10cm (2⅝ x 4in)

Materials
14-count white Aida
16.5 x 20cm (6½ x 8in)
★
Tapestry needle size 24–26
★
DMC stranded cotton (floss)
as listed in chart key
★
Lightweight iron-on interfacing,
approx 33 x 40cm (13 x 16in)
★
Double-sided adhesive tape
★
Optional piece of thin
wadding (batting)
★
Double-fold white card with
7.5 x 10cm (3 x 4in) aperture

1 Prepare the Aida fabric for work, finding and marking the centre (see page 99). Begin cross stitching from the centre of the fabric and the centre of the chart on page 60.

2 Work over one block of Aida, using two strands of stranded cotton (floss) for cross stitch and one strand for backstitch.

3 When all the stitching is complete, apply lightweight iron-on interfacing to the back of the embroidery, fusing in place with a medium iron. Mount into the card blank following the instructions on page 30.

Inspiration
The joyful fairy designs in the birth sampler and card could be used on many small items – perhaps on a Good Luck card to wish exam success or on the cover of a teenager's study notebook.

Good luck befriend thee, son; for, at thy birth,
The fairery ladies danced upon the hearth;
The drowsy nurse hath sworn she did them spie
Come tripping to the room, where thou didst lie,
And, sweetly singing round about thy bed
Strew all their blessings on thy sleeping head.
From 'Vacation Exercise' by John Milton (1608–74)

Memories Album

Preserve all your wonderful memories of a baby's early days in a photograph album covered with this sweet design. If desired, you could easily change the colouring of the border and the word Baby.

Stitch count
74 x 100
Finished size
13.5 x 18cm (5¼ x 7⅛in)

Materials
14-count white Aida
24 x 28cm (9½ x 11in)

★

Tapestry needle size 24–26

★

DMC stranded cotton (floss)
as listed in chart key

★

Lightweight iron-on interfacing,
approx 33 x 40cm (13 x 16in)

★

Double-sided adhesive tape

★

Photograph album at least
15 x 20cm (6 x 8in), ready
covered or covered in
fabric of your choice

1 Prepare the fabric for work, finding and marking the centre (see page 99). Begin stitching from the centre of the fabric and chart on page 62.

2 Work over one block of Aida, using two strands of stranded cotton (floss) for cross stitch and French knots and then one strand for backstitch.

3 When all the stitching is complete, apply lightweight iron-on interfacing to the back of the embroidery to prevent fraying, fusing in place with a medium iron. Trim the embroidery to within four squares of the Aida on all sides and attach it centrally to the front of your photograph album using strips of double-sided tape. Add a ribbon trim if desired.

Inspiration

Work the album design as a door plaque, stitching a name using either the backstitch alphabet on page 63 or letters from the fairy alphabet pages 45–51. (If the name is a long one, extend the edges of the border and move the stars further left.) Use double-sided tape to stick the embroidery to stiff card, folding the edges to the back and fixing in place with tape. Stitch a ribbon loop to the top for a hanger.

*Children born of fairy stock
Never need for shirt or frock,
Never want for food or fire,
Always get their hearts' desire.*

From 'I'd Love to be a Fairy's Child'
by Robert Graves (1895–1985)

Tooth Fairy Pillow

The Tooth Fairy is said to leave a silver coin under a child's pillow in exchange for a shed milk tooth. This charming pillow has a little pocket all ready for the tooth – the perfect place for the 'fairy' to leave a coin in return.

Stitch count
80 x 80

Finished size of design
14.5 x 14.5cm (5¾ x 5¾in)

Finished size of pillow
16.5 x 16.5cm (6½ x 6½in) approx, excluding trim

Materials

14-count white Aida 25.5 x 25.5cm (10 x 10in) for pillow front

★

14-count white Aida 12.7 x 12.7cm (5 x 5in) for tooth pocket

★

Tapestry needle size 24–26

★

DMC stranded cotton (floss) as listed in chart key

★

Lightweight iron-on interfacing, approx 40 x 33cm (16 x 13in)

★

Matching fabric for pillow back, approx 25.5 x 25.5cm (10 x 10in)

★

Double-sided adhesive tape

★

Lightweight iron-on interfacing

★

White ribbon for a hanging loop, approx 1m (1yd)

★

White lace or broderie anglaise for a frill, approx 1m (1yd)

★

Wadding (batting) for padding

1 Prepare the fabric for work, finding and marking the centre (see page 99). Begin stitching the main design on the larger piece of Aida, from the centre of the fabric and the centre of the chart on page 61. Work over one block of Aida, using two strands of stranded cotton (floss) for cross stitch and French knots and one strand for backstitch. Work the pocket design in the centre of the smaller Aida piece.

2 When all the stitching is complete, apply lightweight iron-on interfacing to the back of both stitched pieces to prevent fraying, pressing with a medium iron to fuse into place.

3 Trim the tooth pocket to within three blocks of Aida along the left, right and bottom edges and to within six blocks across the top edge. Fold over the top edge by three blocks and press lightly. Attach the pocket to the pillow front in the position shown on the chart, using backstitch with white thread.

Making Up the Pillow

4 Make up the pillow by first using a sewing machine or backstitch to sew the lace frill (facing inwards) on the right side of the pillow front, positioning it about 2.5cm (1in) away from the design border.

To make the hanging loop, tack (baste) the ends of the ribbon to the right side top edge of the design 4cm (1½in) in from each side. Place the Aida pillow front and backing fabric right sides together and sew together using a sewing machine or backstitch, following the same line of stitching used to attach the frill. Leave the middle of the bottom edge open and turn the pillow right way out. Pad the pillow with wadding (batting) and then oversew the open bottom edge. Snip the ribbon loop in half and tie in a bow.

Child of the pure unclouded brow and dreaming eyes of wonder,
Though time be fleet, and I and thou are half a life asunder,
Thy loving smile will surely hail the love-gift of a fairy-tale.

From *Through the Looking Glass* by Lewis Carroll (1832–98)

that was

the beginning

of fairies...

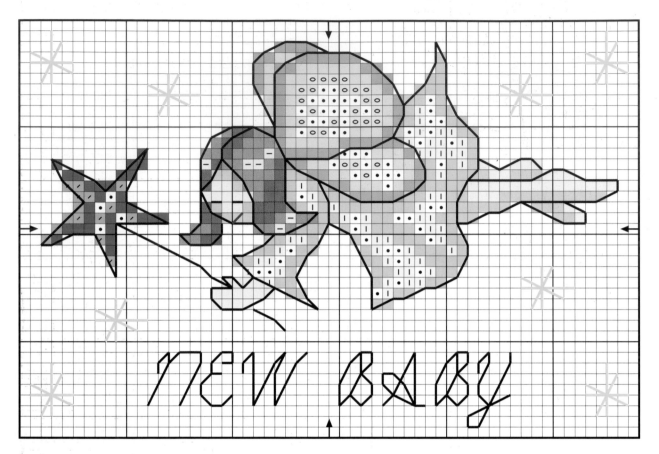

New Baby Card
DMC stranded cotton

Cross stitch

⊙	225			951
	334			3731
	420	✎		3733
	422			3755
—	677			3821
	761	I		3822
	945	•		blanc

Backstitch
— 3799
— 3804
— 3822

The faery beam upon you,
The stars to glisten on you,
A moon of light
In the noon of night,
Till the firedrake hath o'er gone you.

From 'The Faery Beam Upon You' by Benjamin Jonson (1572–1637)

Tooth Fairy

Please

Call ✗ ×

Position of pocket

Tooth Fairy Pillow
DMC stranded cotton

Cross stitch

○ 225 ✓	951 ✓	**Backstitch**	
334 ✓	3731 ✓	— 3799 ✓	
420	3733 ✓	— 3804	
422 ✓	3755 ✓	— 3822	
— 677 ✓	3821 ✓		
761 ✓		3822 ✓	**French knots**
945 ✓	• blanc	● 3799	

420
3733
3804

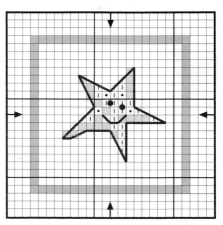

Pocket

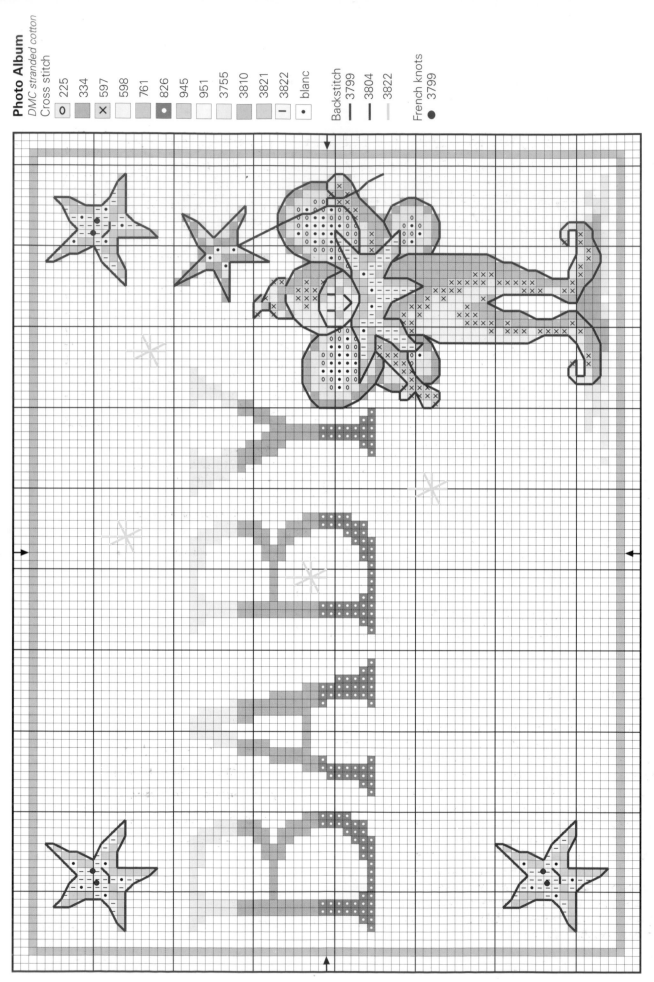

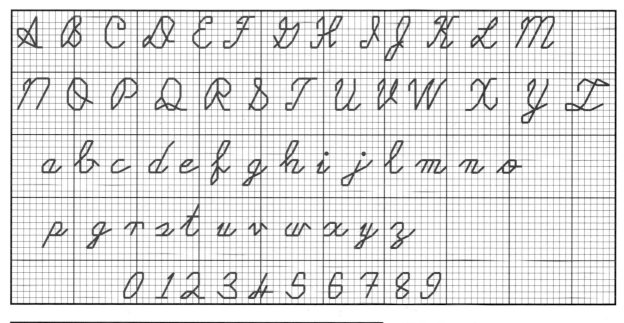

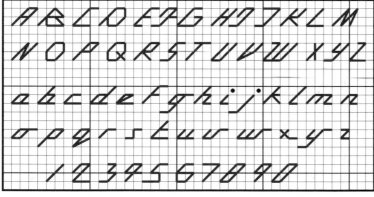

**Birth Sampler
alphabets and numerals**
DMC stranded cotton

Backstitch
— 3799 (or colour of your choice)

French knots
● 3799 (or colour of your choice)

Personalizing Designs

Many of the designs in this book can be easily
personalized by adding names and dates, or even
other messages using the alphabets and numbers
here or a favourite alphabet of your own.

To personalize the Fairy Birth Sampler on page
54, use the small alphabet above to draw out the
name and date on graph paper, making sure the
letters and numbers will fit the heart-shaped space
available. Stitch the text centrally within the space.

If desired, you could use the larger backstitch
alphabet to stitch a completely different poem
for the sampler, planning it out carefully on graph
paper first. There are many lovely fairy poems
featured throughout this book.

*In a utilitarian age, of all
other times, it is a matter of
grave importance that fairy
tales should be respected.*

Charles Dickens (1812–70)

Designed by Joan Elliott

Fairy Godmother

In folklore, fairies are frequently portrayed as helpful to humans, particularly the fairy godmother, who often brought useful advice and good fortune with her. The fairy godmother is a relatively recent introduction, emerging in the 18th century with the publication of the first fairy tales in England. This benevolent character now features in many tales, often appearing at the birth of a child to predict its future or bestow gifts upon it, as in *The Sleeping Beauty*. She also appears at marriages to bring good fortune, or in the case of Cinderella, to make dreams of love come true. Perhaps the real magic of the fairy godmother is showing people their hidden talents and abilities. What dreams can she help you achieve?

Making dreams and wishes come true is the chief function of the fairy godmother and this delightful lady and her little pixies are here to help.

may all your dreams come true

Fairy Godmother Picture

This fun fairy godmother is worked using whole and three-quarter cross stitch, backstitch, long stitch and French knots. The cross stitches on the wings are worked with the addition of a glittering blending filament, while four different colours of seed beads bring an extra magical twinkle to the design.

Stitch count
141 x 186

Design size
25.5 x 33.7cm (10 x 13¼in)

★

Materials

14-count antique white Aida
38 x 46cm (15 x 18in)

★

Tapestry needle size 24
and a beading needle

★

DMC stranded cotton (floss)
as listed in chart key

★

Kreinik Blending Filament
032 pearl (2 spools)

★

Kreinik Fine #8 Braid 005 black

★

Kreinik Very Fine #4 Braid:
028 citron (3 spools) and
102 vatican (2 spools)

★

Mill Hill glass seed beads:
00557 gold; 02010 ice;
02024 heather mauve and
03021 royal pearl

1 Prepare for work, referring to page 99 for Techniques if necessary. Find and mark the centre of the fabric and the centre of the chart. You could mount the fabric in an embroidery frame if you wish.

2 Start stitching from the centre of the chart and fabric, using two strands of stranded cotton (floss) for full and three-quarter cross stitches. Use one strand of Kreinik 005 wrapped twice around the needle for French knots in the lettering and the fairy godmother's eyes. Use one strand of DMC 3371 wrapped once around the needle for the French knots for little pixies' eyes. Following the colour changes on the chart, use one strand wrapped twice around the needle for all other French knots. Use two strands

of Kreinik 028 for the fairy godmother's glasses. Use one strand for all other backstitch and the long stitches in the lettering and the wands.

3 Working in one direction and in half cross stitch, overstitch the completed DMC blanc, 747 and 3756 cross stitches in all the wings with one strand of the pearl Kreinik Blending Filament 032 to create extra glitter. Attach all the different beads where indicated on the chart using a beading needle and matching thread (see Techniques page 100).

4 Once the embroidery is complete, check for missed stitches and then finish your picture by mounting and framing (see page 34).

Inspiration

Choose a 12-count Aida or 24-count linen band with a decorative edge and stitch the narrow side borders from the main chart to create two pretty bookmarks. Omit the beads or work French knots instead. Hem the top and bottom of the band neatly to finish.

I do wander everywhere,
Swifter than the moone's sphere;
And I serve the fairy queen,
To dew her orbs upon the green.

From *A Midsummer-Night's Dream* by William Shakespeare (1564–1616)

Pixie Sachet

This scented sachet features a pixie from the main chart, stitched on 14-count navy Aida, following the stitching instructions opposite. Once complete, trim the embroidery to the required size, with matching backing fabric. With right sides facing, stitch the two pieces together, leaving a gap for turning at the top. Turn through to the right side and stuff with pot-pourri. Insert a loop of cord in the gap and sew in place. Slipstitch decorative cord all around the edges starting at the gap. Tuck the ends into the gap and slipstitch closed. Stitch on two star buttons to finish.

Inspiration

Work just one of the little pixies on 14-count Aida or 28-count linen and mount into a ready-made or homemade card (see page 30 for making cards).

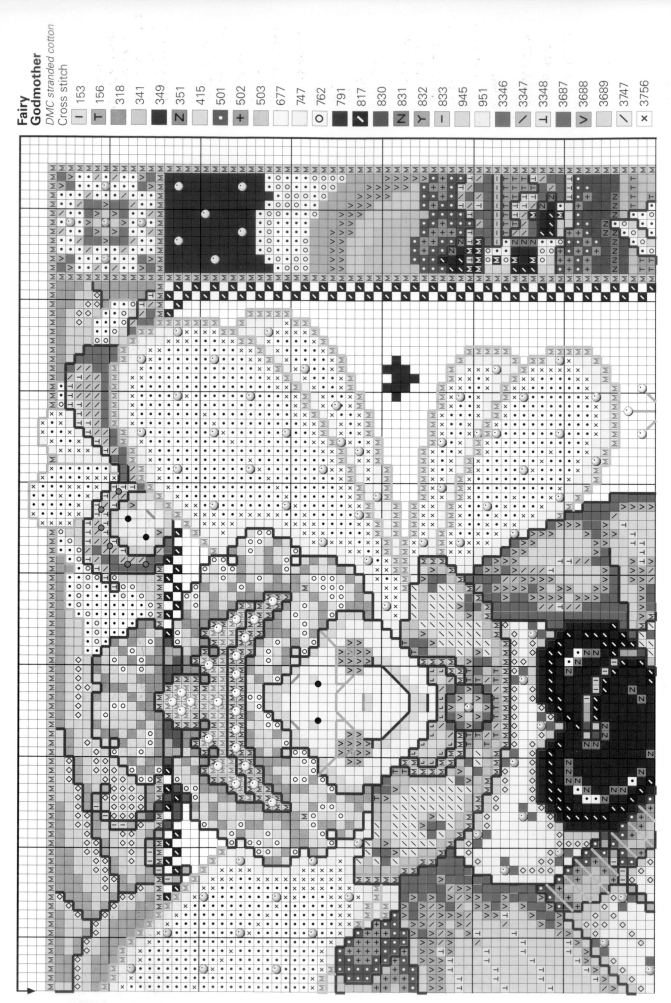

Key:

3771
3820
3822
3835
3836
3852
blanc
Kreinik #4 102
Kreinik #4 028
Kreinik #8 005

Backstitch
831 (noses & eyebrows)
3346
3371
Kreinik #4 102
Kreinik #4 028
Kreinik #8 005

French knots
3346
3687
3835
3852
Kreinik #8 005

Mill Hill seed beads
00557 gold
02010 ice
02024 heather
03021 pearl

Use Kreinik blending filament 032 pearl to work half cross stitches on all wings over the blanc, 747 and 3756 cross stitches

	153	156	318	341	349	351	415	501	502	503	677	747	762	791	817	830	831	832	833	945	951	3346	3347	3348	3687	3688	3689	3747	3756
	−	T			Z			•	+				O		╱	╱	Y	I				╱	T		V		╲	×

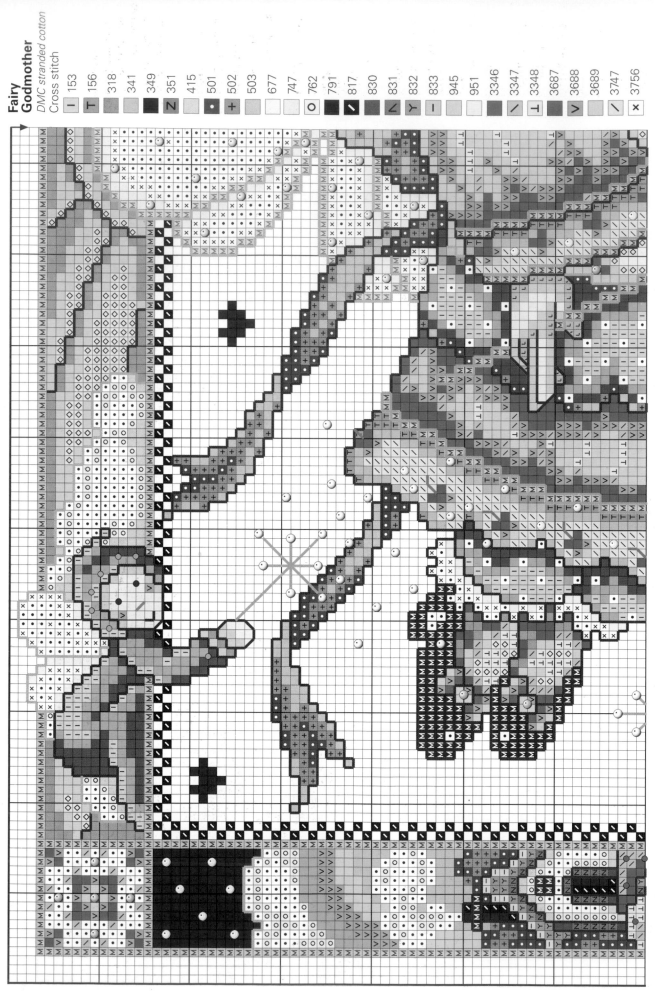

3771
3820
3822
3835
3836
3852
blanc
Kreinik #4 102
Kreinik #4 028
Kreinik #8 005

Backstitch
831 (noses & eyebrows)
3346
3371
Kreinik #4 102
Kreinik #4 028
Kreinik #8 005

French knots
3346
3687
3835
3852
Kreinik #8 005

Mill Hill seed beads
00557 gold
02010 ice
02024 heather
03021 pearl

Use Kreinik blending filament 032 pearl to work half cross stitches on all wings over the blanc, 747 and 3756 cross stitches

Designed by Lesley Teare

Fairy Seasons

Fairies can be seen in all seasons by those who know their haunts or the magic phrases to call them forth, and this delightful collection of collage-style motifs reveals some of their hiding places. In spring, fairies play among meadow flowers, ringing bluebells as a call to play and taking refuge under foxgloves from spring showers. In summer, water nymphs cavort in seas, rivers and ponds, riding fish and dragonflies and sleeping in cozy water lilies. In autumn, dryads dance in woodland glades, dining on berries, riding snails and resting on toadstools. In winter, fairy sprites in festive green and red shelter from snowflakes under holly and ivy and give gifts at Yule time – just like Father Christmas's elves.

Dozens of seasonal fairy motifs in a versatile collage style allow you to mix and match designs and create a wonderful array of projects.

Spring Fairies

Meadow fairies dressed in spring green revel in daffodils, snowdrops, bluebells, violets and foxgloves and decorate a sachet, bowl, bell pull and card. Fairy wings are given a magical glitter with Glissen Gloss thread. Refer to the Spring Fairy charts overleaf and Suppliers on page 103 for sources of items used.

Stitch count
41 x 46

Finished size of motif
7.5 x 8.3cm (3 x 3¼in)

Materials
28-count antique white
Cashel linen 14 x 14cm (5½ x 5½in)

★

Tapestry needle size 24–26

★

DMC stranded cotton (floss)
as listed in chart key

★

Madeira Glissen Gloss thread,
300 rainbow and
Anchor Reflecta thread, 0300 gold

★

Backing fabric to tone with embroidery,
12.5 x 12.5cm (5 x 5in)

★

Polyester filling

★

Narrow ribbon, approx 15cm (6in) long

★

Narrow decorative cord,
approx 51cm (20in) long

★

Tassel (bought or
homemade)

Sachet

1 Stitch the design in the centre of the linen over two threads, using two strands of stranded cotton (floss) for cross stitch and one for backstitch. Cross stitch the wings with one strand of blanc and one of Glissen Gloss together in the needle.

2 Trim the embroidery to 12.5cm (5in) square, to match the backing fabric. Using matching thread stitch a 1.25cm (½in) seam all around, leaving a gap for turning at the top. Turn through to the right side and stuff with polyester filling.

3 Slipstitch the decorative cord all around the edges of the sachet, starting at the gap and tucking the ends into the gap. Fold the ribbon in half, insert it into the gap and slipstitch closed. Stitch on a tassel at the bottom centre to finish (see page 101 for making a simple tassel).

Stitch count
35 x 37

Finished size of motif
6.3 x 6.7cm (2½ x 2⅝in)

Materials
28-count antique white Cashel linen
11 x 11cm (4½ x 4½in)

★

Tapestry needle size 24–26

★

DMC stranded cotton (floss)
as listed in chart key

★

Madeira Glissen Gloss thread,
300 rainbow and
Anchor Reflecta thread, 0300 gold

★

Blue ceramic bowl 9cm (3½in)
diameter (Framecraft)

Bluebell Bowl

1 Stitch the design in the centre of the linen over two threads, working cross stitch with two strands of stranded cotton (floss). Cross stitch the wings with one strand of blanc and one of Glissen Gloss together. Work backstitches in one strand.

2 Mount into the bowl lid following the manufacturer's instructions.

Stitch count
91 x 37
Finished size of motif
16.5cm x 6.7cm (6½ x 2⅝in)

Materials
28-count off-white linen band with
chevron edge (Viking Loom)
26cm (10in) long x 11cm (4in) wide
★
Tapestry needle size 24–26
★
DMC stranded cotton (floss)
as listed in chart key
★
Madeira Glissen Gloss thread,
300 rainbow and
Anchor Reflecta thread, 0300 gold
★
Wooden bell pull ends, cut to size
★
Iron-on interfacing
★
Cord or ribbon for hanging,
approx 20cm (8in)

Their life all pleasure,
and their task all play,
All spring their age,
and sunshine all their day.

From 'To Mrs Priestley with some
drawings of Birds and Insects' by
Anna Laetitia Barbauld (1743–1825)

Bell Pull

1 Oversew the raw edges of the
linen band. Work from the centre of
the motif and the centre of the band,
outwards over two threads, using
two strands of stranded cotton
(floss) for cross stitch and one for
backstitch. Cross stitch the wings with
one strand of blanc and one of Glissen
Gloss together.

2 Iron interfacing on the back of the
band. Turn 2.5cm (1in) under at both
ends and slipstitch in place, leaving the
sides open to slide the bell pull ends
through. Attach cord or ribbon for hanging.

Stitch count
22 x 37
Finished size of motif
4 x 6.7cm (1½ x 2⅝in)

Materials
14-count white Aida
8 x 11cm (3 x 4½in)
★
Tapestry needle size 24–26
★
DMC stranded cotton (floss)
as listed in chart key
★
Madeira Glissen Gloss thread,
300 rainbow and
Anchor Reflecta thread, 0300 gold
★
Double-fold card with oblong aperture
to fit embroidery motif
★
Card for a double mount
★
Double-sided adhesive tape

Spring Card

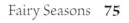

1 Stitch the design in the centre of the
Aida over one block, working cross
stitch with two strands of stranded cotton
(floss). Cross stitch the wings with one
strand of blanc and one of Glissen Gloss
together. Work backstitches in one strand.

2 Make a double-mount card as shown
on page 30 (or buy a ready-made card)
and mount your embroidery in the card.
To add a second mount in a contrasting
colour, as shown here, cut a piece of card
with a smaller aperture than the main card
and use tape to stick it in place behind the
larger aperture.

Spring Fairies

DMC stranded cotton

Cross stitch

✕	156
	164
⊙	310
	333
	340
	676
I	704
	718
	720
	727
	729
	742
O	743
＼	745
	819
	869
	905
	906
Ｏ	915
+	3078
	3607
	3608
	3747
	3823
／	3828
•	blanc
−	blanc (1 strand) + Madeira Glissen Gloss 300 rainbow (1 strand)

Backstitch

▬	350
▬	869
▬	Anchor Reflecta 0300 gold

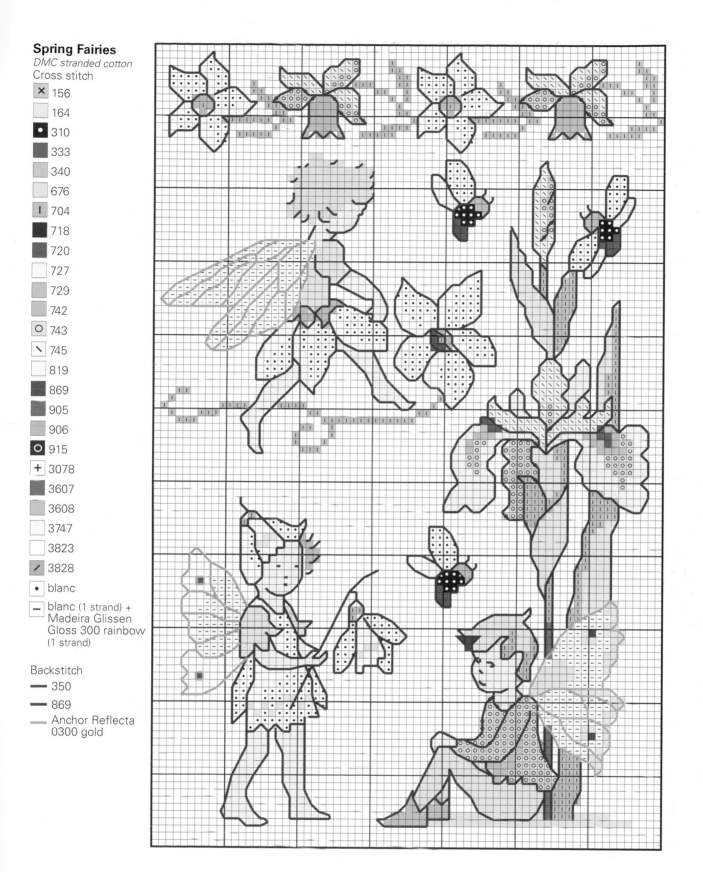

Summer Fairies

At the height of summer, water nymphs play among creatures of the sea, river and pond. The watery motifs have been used to create a towel band, a gift tag and large and small drawstring bags. Fairy wings are given a lovely shimmer with Glissen Gloss thread. Refer to the Summer Fairy charts overleaf and Suppliers on page 103 for sources of the items used.

Towel Band

1 Stitch the design from the centre of the Aida over one block, working cross stitch with two strands of stranded cotton (floss). Cross stitch the wings with one strand of blanc and one of Glissen Gloss together. Work backstitches with one strand. Work the zigzag border along the band, two squares below the motif at the bottom and one square above at the top.

2 When stitching is finished turn all edges under by 1.5cm (½in). Find the centre of the towel and the centre of the band and pin the band 4cm (1½in) from the base of the towel. Slipstitch or machine stitch into place and remove pins.

She rides upon her little boat, her swans swim through the starry sheen, Rowing her into Fairyland The lovely-eyed Evangeline.

From 'The Night Swans' by Walter de la Mare (1873–1953)

Stitch count
(excluding zigzag border)
24 x 28
Finished size of motif
(excluding zigzag border)
4.4 x 5cm (1¾ x 2in)
★
Materials
Small guest or hand towel
★
14-count white Aida fabric 8cm (3¼in) wide x width of the towel plus 1.5cm (½in) for turnings on all edges
★
Tapestry needle size 24–26
★
DMC stranded cotton (floss) as listed in chart key
★
Madeira Glissen Gloss thread, 300 rainbow and Anchor Reflecta thread, 312 blue

Stitch count
17 x 39
Finished size of motif
3 x 7cm (1¼ x 2¾in)

Materials
14-count pale aqua Aida 7 x 11cm (2¾ x 4¼in)
★
Tapestry needle size 24–26
★
DMC stranded cotton (floss) as listed in chart key
★
Stiff card for the tag
★
Double-sided adhesive tape
★
Short length of narrow ribbon

Gift Tag

1 Stitch from the centre of the Aida over one block, using two strands of stranded cotton (floss) for cross stitch and French knots and one for backstitch.

2 Trim the stitching to the required size, fray the edges and secure to the card with double-sided tape. Punch a hole in the card and add the ribbon tie to finish.

Large Drawstring Bag

Stitch count
51 x 53
Finished size of motif
9.2 x 9.6cm (3⅝ x 3¾in)

Materials
14-count pale aqua Aida
18 x 18cm (7 x 7in)

★

Tapestry needle size 24–26

★

DMC stranded cotton (floss)
as listed in chart key

★

Madeira Glissen Gloss thread,
300 rainbow and
Anchor Reflecta thread, 312 blue

★

Two pieces of fabric for the bag,
at least 46 x 25cm (18 x 10in) each

★

Ribbon or cord for a drawstring

★

Four decorative buttons

1 Work from the centre of the Aida over one block, using two strands of stranded cotton (floss) for cross stitch and one for backstitch. Cross stitch the wings with one strand of blanc and one of Glissen Gloss together.

2 Pin the Aida patch on to one of the bag fabric pieces, centrally and about 4cm (1½in) from the bottom. Using matching thread, stitch in place 6mm (¼in) in from the edges to allow for a fringe. Stitch the buttons in the corners, adding further decorative stitching if you wish, and then fray the edges of the patch.

3 Make up the bag by placing the bag pieces right sides together. Leaving 12.5cm (5in) open at the top on both sides, stitch 1.5cm (½in) from the raw edges down one side, along the bottom and up the other side. Trim bottom corners diagonally and press seams open. Turn the top edge over about 11.5cm (4½in) to make a hem and channel for the drawstring, and machine stitch a line 2.5cm (1in) from the folded edge and another about 6.5cm (2½in) further down.

4 Thread a length of ribbon through the casing for the drawstring, join the ends together and conceal in the casing.

Small Drawstring Bag

Stitch count
46 x 38
Finished size of motif
8.3 x 7cm (3¼ x 2¾in)

Materials
Two pieces of 14-count pale aqua
Aida, at least 30 x 20cm (12 x 8in)

★

Tapestry needle size 24–26

★

DMC stranded cotton (floss)
as listed in chart key

★

Madeira Glissen Gloss thread,
300 rainbow and
Anchor Reflecta thread, 312 blue

★

Ribbon or cord for a drawstring

1 The motif is stitched directly on to one of the pieces of Aida; for a different sized bag simply make the pieces larger or smaller. Work from the centre of one of the Aida pieces over one block, using two strands of stranded cotton (floss) for cross stitch and one for backstitch. Cross stitch the wings with one strand of blanc and one of Glissen Gloss together.

2 When stitching is complete trim the fabric pieces to size and oversew all raw edges. Place the two pieces right sides together and, leaving a 5cm (2in) opening at the top on both sides, stitch 1.5cm (½in) from the raw edges down one side, along the bottom and up the other side. Trim the bottom corners diagonally and press side seams open. Turn the top edge over about 3.5cm (1½in) to make a hem and channel for the drawstring, and machine stitch a line 2cm (¾in) from the folded edge and another about 2cm (¾in) further down.

3 Thread a length of ribbon or cord through the casing for a drawstring, join the ends and conceal the join in the casing.

I'll give thee fairies to attend on thee;
And they shall fetch thee jewels fom the deep,
And sing, while thou on pressed flowers doth sleep.

From *A Midsummer-Night's Dream* by William Shakespeare (1564–1616)

Summary Fairies

DMC stranded cotton
Cross stitch

- ◨ 310
- ◼ 517
- ◉ 518
- ▨ 519
- ✚ 728
- ▨ 729
- ▨ 782
- ▢ 819
- ▢ 828
- ▨ 912
- ＼ 954
- ▨ 955
- ▨ 962
- ▨ 963
- ▢ 3078
- ◯ 3326
- • 3819
- ▨ 3853
- ╱ 3854
- ▨ 3855
- − blanc (1 strand) +
  Madeira Glissen
  Gloss 300 rainbow
  (1 strand)
- ▣ Anchor Reflecta
  312 blue (1 strand)

Backstitch
- —— 801
- —— 3328
- —— Anchor Reflecta
  312 blue

French knots
- ◯ 912

Autumn Fairies

In these designs woodland dryads dressed in autumnal colours cavort among fallen leaves and late corn and gather their own harvest of berries. These motifs are used to adorn a notebook, pencil holder, purse and bookmark. Refer to the Autumn Fairy charts overleaf and Suppliers on page 103 for sources of items used.

Stitch count
36 x 66 excluding border
Finished size of motif
6.5 x 12cm (2½ x 4¾in)

Materials
14-count cream Aida band 10cm (4in) wide x width of your book

★

Tapestry needle size 24–26

★

DMC stranded cotton (floss) as listed in chart key

★

Iron-on interfacing

★

Notebook of your choice

★

Double-sided adhesive tape

Decorated Notebook

1 Cut a length of Aida band the width of your book plus 5cm (2in) each side for turnings.

2 Work from the centre of the band over one block, using two strands of stranded cotton (floss) for cross stitch and one for backstitch, completing each motif with a whole leaf. Repeat as necessary. Add a border top and bottom of the band if you wish.

3 When stitching is complete fuse iron-on interfacing to the back of the band. Fix the band in place on the book with double-sided tape. Turn the ends of the band over to the inside of the book and fix using more tape. To neaten the inside cover, cut a piece of card and tape into position.

Stitch counts
40 x 35 max
Finished size of motifs
7.25 x 6.3cm (2⅝ x 2½in) max

Materials
Two pieces of 14-count cream Aida 13 x 13cm (5 x 5in)

★

Tapestry needle size 24–26

★

DMC stranded cotton (floss) as listed in chart key

★

Pencil holder (Framecraft)

Pencil Holder

1 Work the designs from the centre of the Aida pieces over one block, using two strands of stranded cotton (floss) for cross stitch and one for backstitch.

2 Trim the embroideries to fit the pencil holder and mount according to the manufacturer's instructions.

Small Purse

Stitch count
35 x 16
Finished size of motif
6.3 x 3cm (2½ x 1⅛in)

Materials
Two pieces of 28-count cream linen,
approx 18 x 18cm (7 x 7in)

★

Tapestry needle size 24–26

★

DMC stranded cotton (floss)
as listed in chart key

★

Two pieces of cream silk or lining
fabric, approx 18 x 18cm (7 x 7in)

★

Purse clasp
(Viking Loom LCSG27)

★

Glass beads to match clasp

1 Tack (baste) the outline of the bag template provided on page 104 on to both linen pieces. Repeat with the lining fabric, using the smaller lining template.

2 Stitch the design just below the centre of one of the linen pieces, working over two threads and using two strands of stranded cotton (floss) for cross stitch and French knots and one for backstitch.

3 To make up the purse bag, pin the linen pieces right sides together, leaving top edges open and 3cm (1¼in) at either side. Using tacking (basting) lines as a guide, machine sew the pieces together. Repeat with the lining fabric.

4 Remove tacking except along the top (for a guide when hemming the top edge). Repeat with the lining. Press seams and cut V-shaped notches around the corners before turning right side out. Press and notch the lining but leave this right sides together.

5 Place the lining inside the purse bag, matching side openings. Starting with the front, begin to turn the raw edges under so they are sandwiched between the lining and the front, using the tacking (basting) as a guide. Pin in position and repeat with the back. Slipstitch the front and back openings in place, then position the bag to fit inside the purse frame and secure with backstitch.

6 Complete the purse by sewing the beads into the holes at the front of the purse clasp, using two strands of matching cotton (floss) and cross stitch.

Bookmark

Stitch count
49 x 25
Finished size of motif
9 x 4.5cm (3½ x 1¾in)

Materials
14-count cream Aida band with
decorated border (Willow Fabrics)
20.5cm (8in) long x 6.3cm (2½in) wide

★

Tapestry needle size 24–26

★

DMC stranded cotton (floss)
as listed in chart key

★

Double-sided adhesive tape

★

Tassel (bought or homemade)

★

Iron-on interfacing

1 Begin stitching from the base of the design, twenty-four stitches from the bottom of the band, matching the centre of the motif with the centre of the band width. Work over one block, using two strands of stranded cotton (floss) for cross stitch and one for backstitch. To form a decorative point, work cross stitches in DMC 3830 from each side of the band, starting seven rows down from the stitched motif.

2 Fold the bottom edge of the band under, angling each side to create a point and catching at the back with slipstitches. Fold the top over and secure with slipstitches or double-sided tape. Sew the tassel on to the point (see page 101 for making a tassel). To finish, cut a strip of iron-on interfacing and fuse in place at the back of the bookmark.

Autumn Fairies
DMC stranded cotton
Cross stitch

	225
	300
	310
	327
◣	349
	351
O	435
I	437
–	471
	553
	732
×	734
	746
	754
	780
T	822
	832
+	834
◉	918
V	3046
	3047
	3778
–	3830
	3346
	3853
╱	3854
•	blanc

Backstitch
—— 300
—— 310
—— 349

French knots
● 310
● 327

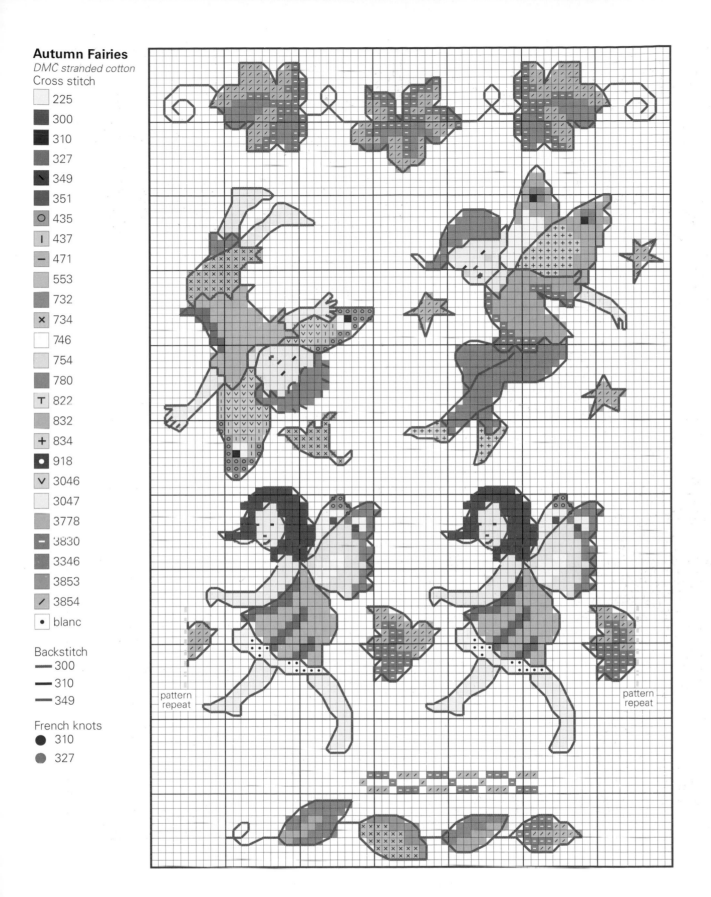

pattern repeat

pattern repeat

Winter Fairies

Among twinkling snowflakes, holly and ivy, winter fairies enjoy the season. These festive motifs have been used to create a Christmas card and holder, a pot and a napkin and holder. Fairy wings are given the glisten of frost with Glissen Gloss thread. Refer to the Winter Fairy charts overleaf and Suppliers on page 103 for sources of items used.

Stitch count
34 x 39
Finished size of motif
6 x 7cm (2⅜ x 2¾in)

Materials
14-count white Aida
15 x 15cm (6 x 6in)

★

Tapestry needle size 24–26

★

DMC stranded cotton (floss)
as listed in chart key

★

Madeira Glissen Gloss thread,
300 rainbow and
Anchor Reflecta thread, 0300 gold

★

Two pieces of stiff card
15 x 15cm (6 x 6in)

★

Wadding (batting) 15 x 15cm (6 x 6in)

★

Cotton Christmas fabric to tone with
embroidery 20 x 20cm (8 x 8in)

★

Double-sided adhesive tape

★

Red satin ribbon
2.5cm (1in) wide x 1m (1yd)

★

Small brass ring

Christmas Card Holder

1 Stitch the design in the centre of the Aida over one block, working cross stitch with two strands of stranded cotton (floss) and backstitch with one. Cross stitch the wings with one strand of blanc and one of Glissen Gloss together.

2 Trim the embroidery to 10cm (4in) square. Place wadding (batting) on top of a 15cm (6in) square of card and the cotton fabric over the wadding. Fold the edges to the back and fix with tape.

3 For a hanger, sew a short length of ribbon to the top of the holder, passing it through a brass ring and stitching in place at the back of the holder. Stitch the remaining length of ribbon centrally to the bottom. Neaten the back by fixing a square of card in place with double-sided tape.

Stitch count
39 x 38
Finished size of motif
7 x 7cm (2¾ x 2¾in)

Materials
14-count white Aida
15 x 15cm (6 x 6in)

★

Tapestry needle size 24–26

★

DMC stranded cotton (floss)
as listed in chart key

★

Madeira Glissen Gloss thread,
300 rainbow and
Anchor Reflecta thread, 0300 gold

★

Ceramic pot 9cm (3½in)
diameter (Framecraft)

Ivy Pot

1 Work the design in the centre of the Aida over one block, working cross stitch with two strands of stranded cotton (floss) and backstitch with one. Cross stitch the wings with one strand of blanc and one of Glissen Gloss together.

2 Mount into the pot lid following the manufacturer's instructions.

Napkin and Holder

Stitch counts
Napkin: 16 x 15
Holder: 24 x 30
Finished sizes of motifs
Napkin: 3 x 2.7cm (1⅛ x 1in)
Holder: 4.3 x 5.5cm (1¾ x 2⅛in)
for one repeat, including border

Materials
for one napkin and holder
14-count white linen
30 x 30cm (12 x 12in) for napkin
16.5 x 9.5cm (6½ x 3¾in) for holder
★
Tapestry needle size 24–26
★
DMC stranded cotton (floss)
as listed in chart key
★
Iron-on interfacing
★
Popper fastener or a small
piece of Velcro

1 To stitch the napkin, hem the linen by 1cm (⅜in) all round. Mitre the corners, machine stitch in place and press hems.

2 Work the motif in one corner, twelve squares from the edges, working over two fabric threads and using two strands of stranded cotton (floss) for cross stitch and one for backstitch.

3 To stitch the holder, zigzag stitch or oversew the linen edges. Working from the centre of the strip and over two threads, stitch two repeats of the motif along the band, using two strands for cross stitch and one for backstitch.

4 Turn a small hem along the top and bottom of the linen strip. Turn over both ends and fuse all folds into place with iron-on interfacing. Sew on a popper fastener or piece of Velcro to fasten the holder around the napkin.

Christmas Card

Stitch count
69 x 47
Finished size of motif
12.5 x 8.5cm (5 x 3⅜in)

Materials
14-count white Aida
20 x 15cm (8 x 6in)
★
Tapestry needle size 24–26
★
DMC stranded cotton (floss)
as listed in chart key
★
Madeira Glissen Gloss thread,
300 rainbow and
Anchor Reflecta thread, 0300 gold
★
Double-fold cream card with
14 x 9cm (5½ x 3½in) aperture
★
Double-sided adhesive tape

1 Work from the centre of the Aida over one block, using two strands of stranded cotton (floss) for cross stitch and then one for backstitch. Cross stitch the wings with one strand of blanc and one of Glissen Gloss together in the needle.

2 When stitching is complete, mount the embroidery in the card (see page 30). Page 30 also has instructions for making your own cards.

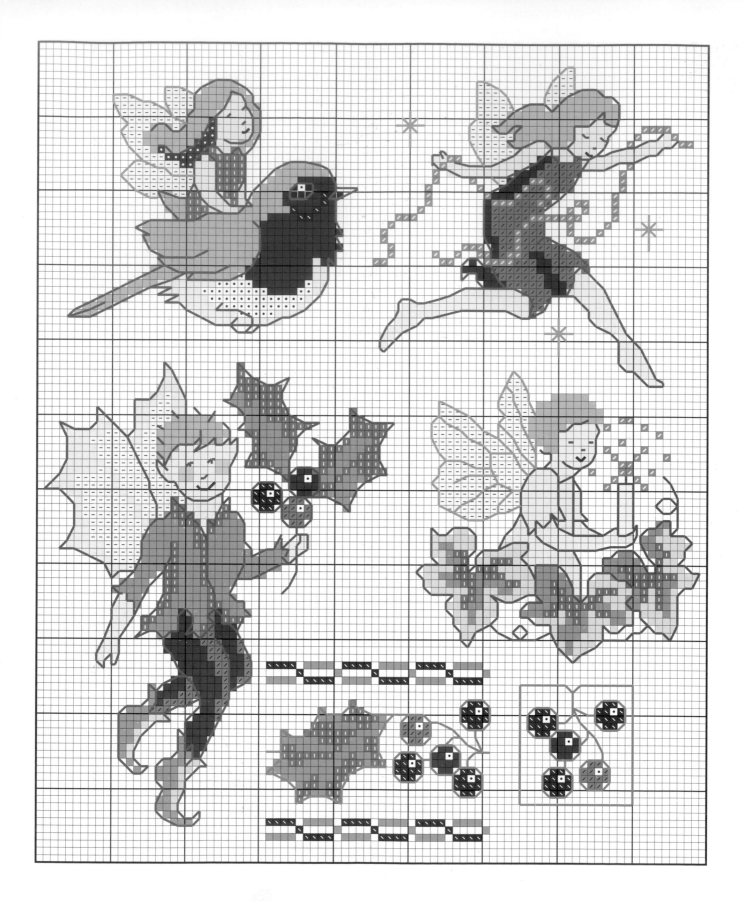

The iron tongue of midnight hath told twelve;
lovers to bed; 'tis almost fairy time.

From *A Midsummer-Night's Dream* by William Shakespeare (1564–1616)

Winter Fairies

DMC stranded cotton

Cross stitch

- 310
- 347
- 369
- 505
- 666
- 680
- 704
- 728
- 746
- 761
- 819
- 869
- 905
- 3756
- 3801
- blanc
- blanc (1 strand) + Madeira Glissen Gloss 300 rainbow (1 strand)
- Anchor Reflecta 0300 gold (1 strand)

Backstitch

- 310
- 869
- 905
- 3801
- Anchor Reflecta 0300 gold

Designed by Lucie Heaton

Fairy Silhouettes

Fairy silhouettes create most attractive designs, as can be seen by this beautiful desk set, where fairies troop in a procession through woodland. Trooping fairies are aristocratic sprites of English folklore who gather to form courts, ruled over by a king and queen, and who sometimes ride out in formal procession. These designs show the closeness of fairies with nature, particularly trees, many of which are sacred to them. The elder is said to offer protection for fairies from evil night spirits. The oak, too, is prized; its acorns can be made into fairy talismans when found by the light of a full moon. Traditionally, the hawthorn was the tree of the Fairy Queen and it was considered unlucky to bring its blossom into the home.

An elegant desk set of paperweight, coaster, bowl, card and journal cover would grace any study while the black on cream colours will suit any décor.

Silhouette Desk Set

Lively fairy designs in dramatic black on cream fabric are perfect for decorating useful office items. The use of the variegated charcoal thread suggests the variable colours of leaves and creates additional depth. The colours can easily be changed, perhaps to dark red on white. See pages 95–97 for the charts and Suppliers on page 103 for details of the items used.

Paperweight

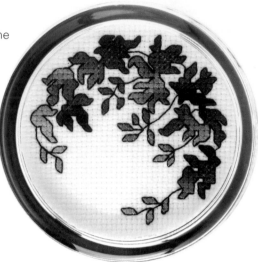

1 Work the design from the centre of the chart and fabric over one block, using two strands of stranded cotton (floss) for full and three-quarter cross stitch and one strand for backstitch.

2 When stitching is complete, back the embroidery by ironing on interfacing to prevent fraying. Trim to fit and mount according to the manufacturer's instructions.

Stitch count
36 x 38
Design size
6.5 x 7cm (2½ x 2¾in)

Materials
14-count cream Aida
18 x 18cm (7 x 7in)
★
Tapestry needle size 24–26
★
DMC stranded cotton (floss),
as listed in chart key
★
Lightweight iron-on interfacing
★
Paperweight 7.6cm (3in)
diameter (Framecraft PW3)

Coaster

1 Work the design from the centre of the chart and the centre of the Aida over one block, using two strands of stranded cotton (floss) for full and three-quarter cross stitch and one strand for backstitch.

2 When all stitching is complete, back the embroidery by ironing on interfacing to prevent fraying. Trim the embroidery to fit the coaster aperture and mount in the coaster according to the manufacturer's instructions.

Stitch count
40 x 39
Design size
7.2 x 7cm (2⅞ x 2¾in)

Materials
14-count cream Aida
18 x 18cm (7 x 7in)
★
Tapestry needle size 24–26
★
DMC stranded cotton (floss),
as listed in chart key
★
Lightweight iron-on interfacing
★
Plastic coaster 8.2cm (3¼in)
diameter (Framecraft CO31)

Trinket Bowl

Stitch count
38 x 43
Design size
7 x 7.8cm (2¾ x 3in)

Materials

14 count cream Aida
18 x 18cm (7 x 7in)
★
Tapestry needle size 24–26
★
DMC stranded cotton (floss),
as listed in chart key
★
Lightweight iron-on interfacing
★
Elm bowl 9cm (3½in)
diameter (Framecraft W4E)

1 Work from the centre of the chart and fabric over one block, using two strands of stranded cotton (floss) for full and three-quarter cross stitch and then one strand for backstitch.

2 Back the embroidery by ironing on the interfacing. Trim to fit the lid and mount according to the manufacturer's instructions.

By the moone we sport and play,
With the night begins our day;
As we daunce, the dew doth fall;
Trip it little urchins all,

From *A Midsummer-Night's Dream* by William Shakespeare (1564–1616)

Greetings Card

Stitch count
41 x 34
Design size
7.4 x 6.2cm (3 x 2½in)

Materials

14-count cream Aida
18 x 18cm (7 x 7in)
★
Tapestry needle size 24–26
★
DMC stranded cotton (floss),
as listed in chart key
★
Optional thin wadding (batting)
★
Double-sided adhesive tape
★
Lightweight iron-on interfacing
★
Double-fold cream card with
8cm (3¼in) aperture

1 Work from the centre of the chart and fabric over one block, using two strands of stranded cotton (floss) for all cross stitches and one for backstitch.

2 Back the embroidery with interfacing, and trim so it is slightly larger than the card aperture. Fix in place with double-sided tape. For a slightly padded look, tape a piece of wadding (batting) behind the embroidery before sealing the card down (see page 30). See page 30 for making your own cards.

Journal Cover

Stitch count
100 x 157
Design size
18 x 28.5cm (7⅛ x 11¼in)

Materials
28-count cream evenweave
33 x 43cm (13 x 17in)

★

Tapestry needle size 24–26

★

DMC stranded cotton (floss),
as listed in chart key

★

Lightweight iron-on interfacing

★

A4-size book or journal
29.7 x 21cm (11½ x 8¼in)
ready-covered or covered in
a fabric of your choice

★

Velvet ribbon for trimming,
1.5cm (½in) wide x
1.5m (1½yd) approx

★

Double-sided adhesive tape

1 Work the design from the centre of the chart and fabric over two threads, using two strands of stranded cotton (floss) for full and three-quarter cross stitch and one strand for backstitch.

2 Iron interfacing on to the back of the embroidery. Trim the fabric to within 2cm (¾in) of the border and stick double-sided tape on the back to the edges of the fabric and from corner to corner. Remove the tape backing and stick the embroidery on to the centre front of your journal.

3 Using more tape, apply velvet ribbon or other trimming over the edges of the embroidery and to the edges of the book, mitring corners neatly. Tuck a small piece of ribbon into the spine of the book to make a matching bookmark.

Inspiration

The large fairy scene would make a delightful framed picture. Try stitching it on a pastel-coloured evenweave or Aida, or one with a metallic sparkle in the weave.

Inspiration

Make a set of placemats using the paperweight design. Stitch on 36-count linen, repeating the design along the side or top edge, turning the motif to create different shapes. Hem the mat or sew a line 2.5cm (1in) inside the edges and fray the edges.

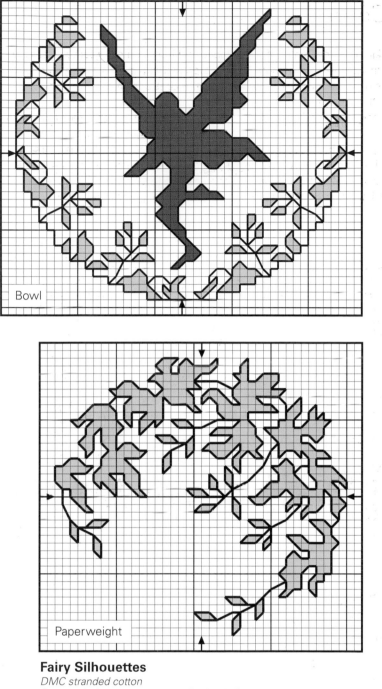

Bowl

Card

Paperweight

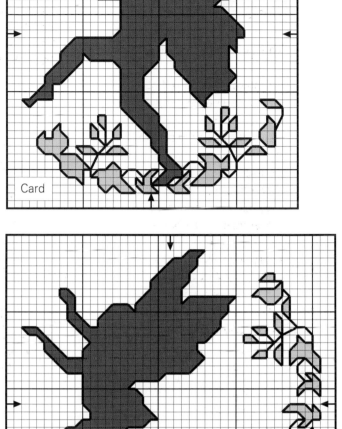

Coaster

Fairy Silhouettes
DMC stranded cotton

Cross stitch

■ 3799

▨ 53 variegated

Backstitch

— 310

In the waning summer light
Which the hearts of mortals love,
'Tis the hour for elphin sprite,
Through the flow'ry mead to rove.

From 'Charlie Among the Elves' by
Edward Knatchbull-Hugessen (1829–93)

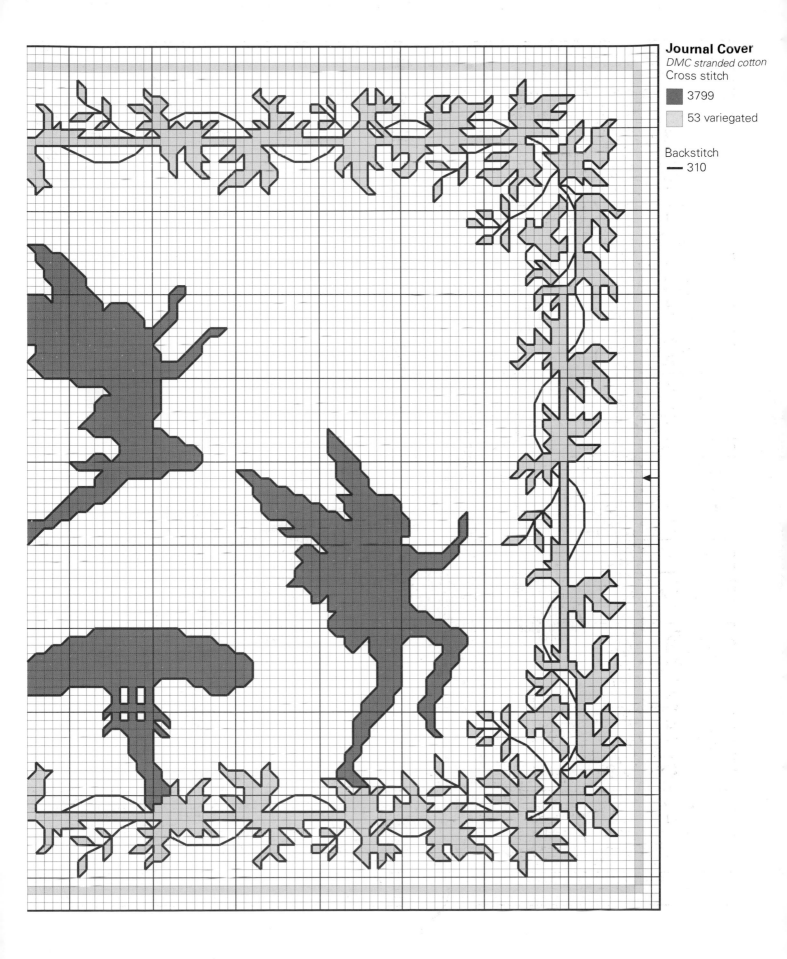

Journal Cover
DMC stranded cotton
Cross stitch

■ 3799

▨ 53 variegated

Backstitch
— 310

Equipment and Techniques

This short but useful section describes the equipment and materials you will need for cross stitch embroidery and the basic techniques and stitches required to work the projects in this book. For beginners there are some handy tips on perfect stitching.

Equipment

Very little equipment is needed for successful cross stitching, which is one of the reasons it's so popular!

Fabrics

The fabrics used for counted cross stitch, mainly Aidas and evenweaves, are woven so they have the same number of threads or blocks to 2.5cm (1in) in both directions. They are available in different counts – the higher the count, the more threads or stitches to 2.5cm (1in), and therefore the finer the fabric.

Aida This is ideal for beginners because the threads are woven in blocks rather than singly. It is available in many fibres, colours and counts and as different width bands. When stitching on Aida, one block on the fabric corresponds to one square on a chart and generally cross stitch is worked over one block.

Evenweaves These are made from linen, cotton, acrylic, viscose, modal and mixtures of all of these, are woven singly and are also available in different colours, counts and bands. To even out any oddities in the weave, cross stitch is usually worked over two threads of the fabric.

Threads

The most commonly used thread for counted embroidery is stranded cotton (floss) but there are many other types available. Many of the projects in this book feature metallic threads and blending filaments to create extra sparkle. The project instructions give how many strands of each thread to use.

You can increase the number of thread colours in your palette by blending or tweeding – that is, combining two or more thread colours in your needle at the same time and working as one to achieve a mottled effect.

Tools

There are many tools and gadgets available for embroidery in craft shops but you really only need the following.

Needles Use blunt tapestry needles for counted cross stitch. The most common sizes used are 24 and 26 but the size depends on the project you are working on and personal preference. Avoid leaving a needle in the fabric unless it is gold plated or it may cause marks. A beading needle (or fine 'sharp' needle), which is much thinner, will be needed to attach beads.

Scissors Use sharp dressmaker's shears for cutting your fabrics and a small, sharp pair of pointed scissors for cutting your embroidery threads.

Frames and hoops These are not essential but if you use one, choose one large enough to hold the complete design to avoid marking the fabric and flattening your stitches.

Basic Techniques

The following pages describe how to prepare fabric, how to use the charts and keys and how to work the stitches.

Preparing Fabric for Work

Press embroidery fabric before you begin stitching and trim the selvedge or any rough edges. Work from the middle of the fabric and the middle of the chart to ensure your design is centred on the fabric. Find the middle of the fabric by folding it in four and pressing lightly. Mark the folds with tailor's chalk or tacking (basting) stitches following a fabric thread. When working with linen sew a narrow hem around all raw edges to preserve them for finishing later.

Stitch Count and Design Size

Each project gives details of the stitch count and finished design size but if you wish to work the design on a different count fabric you will need to be able to calculate the finished size. Count the number of stitches in the design and divide this by the fabric count number, e.g., 140 stitches x 140 stitches ÷ by 14-count = a design size of 10 x 10in (25.4 x 25.4cm). Remember that working on evenweave usually means working over two threads not one, so divide the fabric count by two before you start.

Using the Charts

The designs in this book are worked from colour charts, with symbols where necessary. Each square, both occupied and unoccupied, represents two threads of linen or one block of Aida. Each occupied square equals one stitch. Some designs use three-quarter cross stitches, shown as a triangle within a grid square. Some designs use French knots and beads and these are labelled in the key.

Starting and Finishing Stitching

Unless indicated otherwise, begin stitching in the middle of a design to ensure an adequate margin for making up. Start and finish stitching neatly, avoiding knots which create lumps.

Knotless loop start This neat start can be used with any even number of strands. To stitch with two strands, begin with one strand about 80cm (30in). Double it and thread the needle with the two ends. Put the needle up through the fabric from the wrong side, where you intend to begin stitching, leaving the loop at the back. Form a half cross stitch, put the needle back through the fabric and through the loop to anchor the stitch.

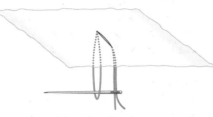

A knotless loop start

Away waste knot start Start this way if using an odd number of strands or when tweeding threads. Thread your needle with the strands required and knot the end. Insert the needle into the right side of the fabric some way away from where you wish to begin stitching. Stitch towards the knot and cut it off when the threads are anchored. Alternatively, snip off the knot, thread the needle and work under a few stitches to anchor the thread.

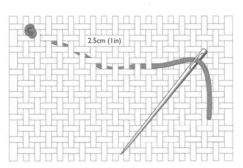

An away waste knot start

Finishing stitching At the back of the work, pass the needle and thread under several stitches of the same or similar colour, and then snip off the thread close to the stitching. You can begin a new colour in a similar way.

Working the Stitches

The projects in the book use basic stitches that are easy to work: simply follow the instructions and diagrams below and overleaf.

Backstitch

Backstitch is used for outlining a design or part of a design, to add detail or emphasis, or for lettering. It is added after the cross stitch has been completed so the backstitch line isn't broken by cross stitches. It is shown on charts by solid coloured lines.

Follow the numbered sequence in the diagram below, working the stitches over one block of Aida or over two threads of evenweave, unless stated otherwise.

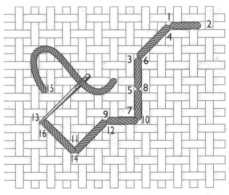

Backstitch

Cross Stitch

This is the most commonly used stitch in this book and can be worked singly or in two journeys. For neat stitching, keep the top stitch facing the same direction. Half cross stitch is simply a single diagonal line.

Cross stitch on Aida Cross stitch on Aida fabric is normally worked over one block of the fabric. To work a complete cross stitch, follow the numbered sequence in the diagram overleaf: bring the needle up through the fabric at 1, cross one block of the fabric and insert the needle at 2. Push the needle through and bring it up at 3, ready to complete the stitch at 4. To work the adjacent stitch, bring the needle up at the bottom right-hand corner of the first stitch.

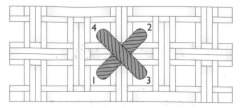

Single cross stitch on Aida fabric

To work cross stitches in two journeys, work the first leg of the cross stitch as above but instead of completing the stitch, work the adjacent half stitch and continue on to the end of the row. Complete all the crosses by working the other diagonals on the return journey.

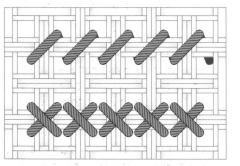

Cross stitch in rows on Aida fabric

Cross stitch on evenweave

This is usually worked over two fabric threads in each direction to even out any oddities in the thickness of the fibres. Bring the needle up to the left of a vertical thread and work your cross stitch in two directions, in a sewing movement, half cross stitch in one direction and then back to cover the original stitches with the second row. This forms single vertical lines on the back and gives somewhere to finish raw ends.

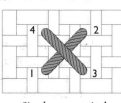

Single cross stitch on evenweave

Three-quarter Cross Stitch

This fractional stitch can produce the illusion of curves. The stitch can be formed on Aida or evenweave but is more successful on evenweave. Three-quarter cross stitch is shown on the charts by a triangle (a half square).

Work the first half of a cross stitch as usual. Work the second 'quarter' stitch over the top and down into the central

hole to anchor the first half of the stitch. If using Aida, you will need to push the needle through the centre of a block of the fabric. Where two three-quarter stitches lie back-to-back in the space of one full cross stitch, work both of the respective quarter stitches into the central hole.

Three-quarter cross stitches on evenweave

French Knot

French knots are small but important little stitches which are predominantly used for eyes and to add detail to a design. They are shown on the charts as coloured circles, with the thread code in the key.

Bring the needle through to the front of the fabric and wind the thread around the needle twice. Begin to push the needle partly through to the back, one thread or part of a block away from the entry point. (This will stop the stitch being pulled to the wrong side.) Gently pull the thread you have wound so it sits snugly at the point where the needle enters the fabric. Pull the needle through to the back and you should have a perfect knot in position. For bigger French knots, it is best to add more strands of thread to the needle rather than winding more times.

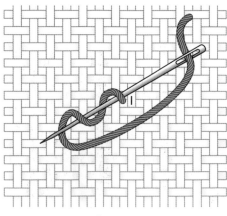

Starting to form a French knot

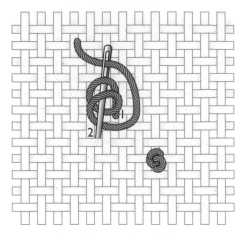

Completing a French knot

Long Stitch

Long straight stitches are used in some of the designs, for example the glittering stars in the Fairy Princess design. They are very simple to stitch and can be worked on any fabric. Simply bring the needle and thread up where the long stitch is to start, at 1 in the diagram below, and down where the chart indicates it should finish, at 2.

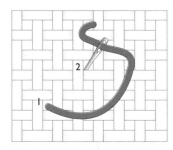

Long stitch

Working with Beads

Some of the designs in the book use beads to bring an extra sparkle and dimension to the design. Beads are shown on the charts as a large coloured circle with a dot, with details of the bead type in the key. You might find using a frame or hoop helpful to keep the fabric taut. Attach beads using a beading needle or very fine 'sharp' needle, thread that matches the bead colour and a half cross stitch (or full cross stitch if you prefer).

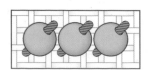

Attaching beads

Making Up

The designs in this book have been made up in many different ways, as described in the project instructions. There are also many 'Inspirations' throughout for other ways to use the versatile designs and display your work to best effect.

Making cards and mounting in cards – see page 30 and 31.

Mounting work as a framed picture – see page 34.

Making up a wall hanging – see page 9.

Making up as a drawstring bag – see page 79.

Making up as a sachet – see pages 67 or 74.

Making a Tassel

Cut a rectangular piece of stiff card, about 1.5cm (½in) longer than the desired size of the tassel. Choose a thread colour to match your project and wrap thread around the card to the desired thickness. Slide the threads off the card, slip a length of thread through the top and tie in a knot. Bind the top third of the tassel with another length of thread and trim all the tassel ends to the same length.

Perfect Stitching

Organize your threads before you start a project as this will help to avoid confusion later. Put threads on an organizer (available from craft shops) and always include the manufacturer's name and the shade number.

★

Separate the strands on a skein of stranded cotton (floss) before taking the number you need, realigning them and threading your needle.

★

When stitching with metallic threads, work with shorter lengths, about 30cm (12in) to avoid tangling and excessive wear on the thread.

★

If using a frame, avoid placing a hoop over the design area as it will stretch the fabric and leave a mark that may be difficult to remove.

★

Plan your route carefully around a chart, counting over short distances wherever possible to avoid making mistakes.

★

Work your cross stitch in two directions in a sewing movement – half cross stitch in one direction and then cover those original stitches with the second row. This forms vertical lines on the back and gives somewhere to finish off raw ends tidily. For neat work the top stitches should all face the same direction.

★

If adding a backstitch outline, always add it after the cross stitch has been completed to prevent the solid line being broken.

The designs in this book use DMC stranded cotton (floss). This DMC/Anchor thread conversion chart is only a guide, as exact colour comparisons cannot always be made. An asterisk * indicates an Anchor shade that has been used more than once so take care to avoid duplication in a design. If you wish to use Madeira threads, telephone for a conversion chart on 01765 640003 or email: acts@madeira.co.uk

DMC	Anchor	DMC	Anchor	DMC	Anchor	DMC	Anchor	DMC	Anchor	DMC	Anchor	DMC	Anchor	DMC	Anchor
B5200	1	355	1014	604	55	781	308*	912	209	3023	899	3765	170	3846	1090
white	2	356	1013*	605	1094	782	308*	913	204	3024	388*	3766	167	3847	1076*
ecru	387*	367	216	606	334	783	307	915	1029	3031	905*	3768	779	3848	1074*
150	59	368	214	608	330*	791	178	917	89	3032	898*	3770	1009	3849	1070*
151	73	369	1043	610	889	792	941	918	341	3033	387*	3772	1007	3850	188*
152	969	370	888*	611	898*	793	176*	919	340	3041	871	3773	1008	3851	186*
153	95*	371	887*	612	832	794	175	920	1004	3042	870	3774	778	3852	306*
154	873	372	887*	613	831	796	133	921	1003*	3045	888*	3776	1048*	3853	1003*
155	1030*	400	351	632	936	797	132	922	1003*	3046	887*	3777	1015	3854	313
156	118*	402	1047*	640	393	798	146	924	851	3047	887	3778	1013*	3855	311*
157	120*	407	914	642	392	799	145	926	850	3051	845*	3779	868	3856	347
158	178	413	236*	644	391	800	144	927	849	3052	844	3781	1050	3857	936*
159	120*	414	235*	645	273	801	359	928	274	3053	843	3782	388*	3858	1007
160	175*	415	398	646	8581*	806	169	930	1035	3064	883	3787	904*	3859	914*
161	176	420	374	647	1040	807	168	931	1034	3072	397	3790	904*	3860	379*
162	159*	422	372	648	900	809	130	932	1033	3078	292	3799	236*	3861	378
163	877	433	358	666	46	813	161*	934	852*	3325	129	3801	1098	3862	358*
164	240*	434	310	676	891	814	45	935	861	3326	36	3802	1019*	3863	379*
165	278*	435	365	677	361*	815	44	936	846	3328	1024	3803	69	3864	376
166	280*	436	363	680	901*	816	43	937	268*	3340	329	3804	63*	3865	2*
167	375*	437	362	699	923*	817	13*	938	381	3341	328	3805	62*	3866	926*
168	274*	444	291	700	228	818	23*	939	152*	3345	268*	3806	62*	48	1207
169	849*	445	288	701	227	819	271	943	189	3346	267*	3807	122	51	1220*
208	110	451	233	702	226	820	134	945	881	3347	266*	3808	1068	52	1209*
209	109	452	232	703	238	822	390	946	332	3348	264	3809	1066*	57	1203*
210	108	453	231	704	256*	823	152*	947	330*	3350	77	3810	1066*	61	1218*
211	342	469	267*	712	926	824	164	948	1011	3354	74	3811	1060	62	1202*
221	897*	470	266*	718	88	825	162*	950	4146	3362	263	3812	188	67	1212
223	895	471	265	720	326	826	161*	951	1010	3363	262	3813	875*	69	1218*
224	895	472	253	721	324	827	160	954	203*	3364	261	3814	1074	75	1206*
225	1026	498	1005	722	323*	828	9159	955	203*	3371	382	3815	877*	90	1217*
300	352	500	683	725	305*	829	906	956	40*	3607	87	3816	876*	91	1211
301	1049*	501	878	726	295*	830	277*	957	50	3608	86	3817	875*	92	1215*
304	19	502	877*	727	293	831	277*	958	187	3609	85	3818	923*	93	1210*
307	289	503	876*	729	890	832	907*	959	186	3685	1028	3819	278	94	1216
309	42	504	206*	730	845*	833	874*	961	76*	3687	68	3820	306	95	1209*
310	403	517	162*	731	281*	834	874*	962	75*	3688	75*	3821	305*	99	1204
311	148	518	1039	732	281*	838	1088	963	23*	3689	49	3822	295*	101	1213*
312	979	519	1038	733	280	839	1086	964	185	3705	35*	3823	386	102	1209*
315	1019*	520	862*	734	279	840	1084	966	240	3706	33*	3824	8*	103	1210*
316	1017	522	860	738	361*	841	1082	970	925	3708	31	3825	323*	104	1217*
317	400	523	859	739	366	842	1080	971	316*	3712	1023	3826	1049*	105	1218*
318	235*	524	858	740	316*	844	1041	972	298	3713	1020	3827	311	106	1203*
319	1044*	535	401	741	304	869	375	973	290	3716	25	3828	373	107	1203*
320	215	543	933	742	303	890	218	975	357	3721	896	3829	901*	108	1220*
321	47	550	101*	743	302	891	35*	976	1001	3722	1027	3830	5975	111	1218*
322	978	552	99	744	301	892	33*	977	1002	3726	1018	3831	29	112	1201*
326	59*	553	98	745	300	893	27	986	246	3727	1016	3832	28	113	1210*
327	101*	554	95	746	275	894	26	987	244	3731	76*	3833	31*	114	1213*
333	119	561	212	747	158	895	1044*	988	243	3733	75*	3834	100*	115	1206*
334	977	562	210	754	1012	898	380	989	242	3740	872	3835	98*	121	1210*
335	40*	563	208	758	9575	899	38	991	1076	3743	869	3836	90	122	1215*
336	150	564	206*	760	1022	900	333	992	1072	3746	1030	3837	177	124	1210*
340	118	580	924	761	1021	902	897*	993	1070	3747	120	3838	177	125	1213*
341	117*	581	281*	762	234	904	258	995	410	3750	1036	3839	176*	126	1209*
347	1025	597	1064	772	259*	905	257	996	433	3752	1032	3840	120*		
349	13*	598	1062	775	128	906	256*	3011	856	3753	1031	3841	159*		
350	11	600	59*	776	24	907	255	3012	855	3755	140	3842	164*		
351	10	601	63*	778	968	909	923*	3013	853	3756	1037	3843	1089*		
352	9	602	57	779	380*	910	230	3021	905*	3760	162*	3844	410*		
353	8*	603	62*	780	309	911	205	3022	8581*	3761	928	3845	1089*		

Suppliers

UK

The American Way
30 Edgbaston Road, Smethwick,
West Midlands B66 4LQ
tel: 0121 601 5454
*For Mill Hill buttons, charms, wire
hangers and many other supplies*

Coats Crafts UK
PO Box 22, Lingfield Estate,
McMullen Road, Darlington,
County Durham DL1 1YQ
tel: 01325 365457 (for a list of stockists)
*For Anchor stranded cotton (floss) and
other embroidery supplies (Coats also
supply some Charles Craft products)*

Craft Creations Limited
1C Ingersoll House, Delamare Road,
Cheshunt, Herts EN8 9HD
tel: 019992 781900
www.craftcreations.com
*For greetings card blanks and
card-making accessories*

From Debbie Cripps
31 Lower Whitelands, Radstock,
Bath BA3 3JW
www.debbiecripps.co.uk
*For buttons, charms and
embroidery supplies*

Dee Fine Arts
182 Telegraph Road, Heswall,
Wirral CH60 0AJ
tel: 0151 3426657
For expert embroidery and picture framing

DMC Creative World
Pullman Road, Wigston,
Leicestershire LE18 2DY
tel: 0116 281 1040
fax: 0116 281 3592
www.dmc/cw.com
*For a huge range of threads, fabrics
and needlework supplies*

Framecraft Miniatures Ltd
Unit 3, Isis House, Lindon Road,
Brownhills, West Midlands WS8 7BW
tel/fax (UK): 01543 360842
tel (international): 44 1543 453154
email: sales@framecraft.com
www.framecraft.com
*For Mill Hill beads, buttons, charms,
wooden and ceramic trinket pots,
notebook covers and many other pre-
finished items with cross stitch inserts*

The Viking Loom
22 High Petergate, York YO1 7EH
tel/fax: 01904 765599
www.vikingloom.co.uk
*For a wide range of needlecraft
products including purse frames,
bell pulls and linen bands*

Willow Fabrics
95 Town Lane, Mobberley, Knutsford,
Cheshire WA16 7HH
Tel freephone (UK): 0800 0567811
(elsewhere): #44 (0) 1565 87 2225
www.willowfabrics.com
*For embroidery fabrics, bands
and Madeira threads*

USA

Market Square Ltd
Wing Farm, Longbridge, Deverill,
Warminster, Wiltshire BA12 7DD
tel: 01985 841041
fax: (520) 888 1483
For wooden boxes

Charles Craft Inc
PO Box 1049
Laurinburg, NC 28353
tel: 910 844 3521
email: ccraft@carolina.net
www.charlescraft.com
*Needlecraft threads and fabrics and
pre-finished items for embroidery*

Design Works Crafts Inc
170 Wilbur Place
Bohemia, New York 11716
tel: 631 244 5749
fax: 631 244 6138
email: customerservice@designworks
crafts.com
*For card mounts and cross stitch
kits of Joan Elliott designs*

Gay Bowles Sales Inc
PO Box 1060
Janesville, WI 53546
tel: 608 754 9212
fax: 608 754 0665
email: millhill@inwave.com
www.millhill.com
*For Mill Hill beads and a US source
for Framecraft products*

Kreinik Manufacturing Company Inc
3106 Timanus Lane, Suite 101
Baltimore, MD 21244
tel: 1800 537 2166
email: kreinik@kreinik.com
www.kreinik.com
*For a wide range of metallic threads
and blending filaments*

The WARM Company
954 East Union Street
Seattle, WA 98122
tel: 1 800 234 WARM
www.warmcompany.com
UK Distributor: W. Williams & Sons Ltd
tel: 017 263 7311
*For polyester filling, cotton wadding
(batting) and Steam-a-Seam fusible web*

Zweigart/Joan Toggit Ltd
262 Old Brunswick Road, Suite E,
Piscataway, NJ 08854-3756
tel: 732 562 8888
email: info@zweigart.com
www.zweigart.com
*For cross stitch fabrics
and pre-finished table linens*

About the Designers

Claire Crompton

Claire studied knitwear design at college before joining the design team at DMC, and finally going freelance. Claire's work has appeared in several magazines, including *Cross Stitch Magic*. Her designs also feature in four David & Charles books: *Cross Stitch Greetings Cards*, *Cross Stitch Alphabets*, *Cross Stitch Angels* and *Cross Stitch Card Collection*. She is currently working on her new book *Cross Stitch Pets*. Claire lives in the Tamar valley, Cornwall, UK.

Joan Elliott

Joan's creations have been enchanting cross stitch enthusiasts the world over for years and she is a leading artist for Design Works Crafts Inc. Her debut book for David & Charles, *A Cross Stitcher's Oriental Odyssey* was followed by *Cross Stitch Teddies* and *Cross Stitch Sentiments and Sayings*. She is currently working on her next book, *Native American Cross Stitch*. Joan lives in America and divides her time between New York and Vermont, USA.

Maria Diaz

Maria studied fine art and painting at university. She then became DMC's first in-house designer, before working as a specialist consultant on a craft publication. Her work appears regularly in craft magazines. Maria has contributed to four previous David & Charles titles: *Cross Stitch Alphabets*, *Cross Stitch Greetings Cards*, *Cross Stitch Myth and Magic* and *Cross Stitch Angels*. Maria lives in Staffordshire, UK.

Lucie Heaton

Lucie studied art, design and textiles at art college. Her longstanding passion for needlework and crafts led her to become a freelance cross stitch designer and over the past ten years her designs have appeared in many of the cross stitch magazines. She has also contributed designs to DMC Creative World and to two books, including *Cross Stitch Alphabets* by David & Charles. Lucie works from home in Nantwich, Cheshire, UK.

Lesley Teare

Lesley trained as a textile designer, with a degree in printed and woven textiles. For some years she has been one of DMC's leading designers and her designs have also featured in many of the cross stitch magazines. Lesley has contributed to three other books for David & Charles, *Cross Stitch Greetings Cards*, *Cross Stitch Alphabets* and *Cross Stitch Angels*. Her book *101 Weekend Cross Stitch Gifts* has just been published. Lesley lives in Hitcham, Suffolk, UK.

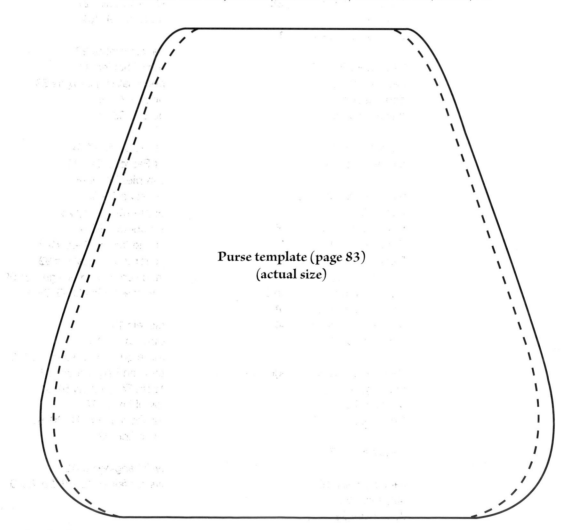

Purse template (page 83)
(actual size)

Acknowledgments

The publishers would like to thank the following people for their magical contributions: Claire Crompton, Maria Diaz, Joan Elliott, Lucie Heaton and Lesley Teare.

Additional thanks to Lin Clements for managing and editing the project and for preparing the charts, and to Kim Sayer and Karl Adamson for the photography.

Thanks to Craft Creations for supplying card blanks and to DMC for supplying fabrics and threads to Maria Diaz.

Index